News
to
Me

News to Me

Adventures of an Accidental Journalist

....

Laurie Hertzel

University of Minnesota Press

Minneapolis · London

Published by the University of Minnesota Press
111 Third Avenue South, Suite 290
Minneapolis, MN 55401-2520
http://www.upress.umn.edu

Design and production by Mighty Media, Inc.
Text design by Chris Long

Library of Congress Cataloging-in-Publication Data

Hertzel, Laurie.
    News to me : adventures of an accidental journalist / Laurie Hertzel.
        p.   cm.
    ISBN 978-0-8166-6558-7 (hc : alk. paper)
    1. Hertzel, Laurie.   2. Journalists—United States—Biography.   I. Title.
    PN4874.H4745A3 2010
    070.92—dc22
    [B]

                                                                2010010388

Printed in the United States of America on acid-free paper

The University of Minnesota is an equal-opportunity educator and employer.

17 16 15 14 13 12 11 10   10 9 8 7 6 5 4 3 2 1

....

In memoriam:

Leo J. Hertzel
Kristin Hertzel Young
Eleanora McCorison

....

Contents

A Storyteller Is Born

I WAS ELEVEN OR TWELVE WHEN I DECIDED THAT JOUR-
nalism was my future. I loved to write, I loved to snoop, I
always wanted to know everything first. Those are pretty
much the only qualifications, when you get right down to it.
Being only eleven or twelve, I had no immediate job oppor-
tunities, but I didn't let that stop me. I launched my own
paper and called it, with the imagination of a true journalist, "Newspaper." The circulation of this fabulous rag was
approximately ten—my immediate family on East Fourth
Street in Duluth. I briefly thought I might make a little
money (a common mistake of young journalists) and tried
to charge them for reading it. Lacking a printing press or a
Xerox machine, I produced one copy of each issue and trotted around the house handing it to various family members,
trying to wheedle a nickel out of them. I may even have
started at a dime and then lowered the price. I don't remember. What I do remember, though, is that whatever the price
was, nobody paid. Eventually, I just tacked my newspaper
onto the bulletin board in the kitchen and spied around the
corner to see if anybody took it down to read.

My entrepreneurial little brothers knew a good idea
when they saw one, and they quickly outflanked me. They

were smarter, they were cuter, and there were two of them, being twins and all. So after the first couple of issues of "Newspaper" came out (stolid and gray, handprinted by yours truly, carefully mimicking the leggy style of professional newspapers, with those long skinny columns of type), my brothers launched a rival paper. Having twice as many brains to work with, they came up with a better concept. Their publication was called "Magapaper"—half newspaper, half magazine. Theirs was in color, damn them. They used crayons. Their stories were shorter (much shorter), and they drew lots of pictures. It was *USA Today*, twenty years ahead of its time.

Their paper caused a brief flurry of excitement in the house, but I am nothing if not stubborn, and I grimly outlasted them. Tony and Tommy went on to other pursuits (primarily, building a fort in the backyard) while I continued my weekly drudgery, churning out my earnest publication for months before letting it wither away. All issues are long since lost, and I remember only one story, a screaming banner headline that shouted, MARGO FLUEGEL HAS ANOTHER BIRTHDAY! Margo Fluegel being my best friend at the time. As you can see, I was well suited for daily journalism; reporting on my friend's birthday was eerily similar to the editor-hits-pothole assignment that I encountered later in my career, and which all reporters dread.

With the demise of "Newspaper," my career in journalism languished, but my passion for writing did not. I began sneaking over to my sister Nancy's desk (off limits, of course, even though we shared a bedroom) and composing stories on her lumpy little Remington Rand. The faster the ideas flowed, the faster I typed, until the keys jammed and

I had to stop and pull them apart with inky fingers. When Nancy discovered me, I escaped with my life but was forced to revert to pencil, and from then on spent hours each day filling up reams of homework paper with laborious semi-plagiarisms of *Anne of Green Gables* and the magical tales of Edward Eager.

In high school, I wrote copy for the yearbook and joined the literary magazine, *The Open Mind*, winning its fiction competition with a story that turned on a pun. ("Jo the Safe" was the tale of a large metal safe who was envious of the silken beauty of a South Asian garment but who, after a tragic fire, came to the conclusion that it was better to be safe than sari.) The prize was five dollars and publication, but Mr. Burrows, the tea-drinking faculty advisor, disapproved. He had been hoping, I think, for a more sophisticated winner.

When people asked me what I was going to do when I grew up, I told them I was going to go live in a cabin in the north woods of Canada with a bunch of cats, and write. Newspapers slipped my mind . . . until 1976, when I was nineteen and looking for full-time work.

For years I had had an after-school job in the stately old Carnegie library in downtown Duluth. There, I shelved books, tidied the stacks, and sometimes helped children choose something to read. For this, I earned seventy-five cents an hour. I loved the library and its long wooden tables, stained-glass windows, and serious high-backed chairs. I loved the studious hush of the second floor, and the happy chatter of the first-floor children's room, where I worked. As a child, I had spent many a sunny afternoon there, tagging along with my mother on her Saturday excursions. Each week, after picking out an armload of fairy tales, I went in search of her, climbing the marble steps to the soaring domed rotunda, usually ending up in the back, in the dim, two-level nook that housed the biographies and the Hans Holzer ghost books. The nook had a cloudy glass ceiling and a narrow wrought-iron staircase, and when I looked up, I could see, through the glass, the feet of the people browsing on the level above.

When I was fourteen, the library gave me a job shelving books, work that I found tedious at best. I used to slip away from my duties as often as I could, threading through the rabbit warren of musty back hallways and storage rooms to the workshop where sweet, elderly Millie mended damaged books with rolls of colored tape and pots of glue. I leaned on the warped wooden table and watched her stitch the signatures back together on an ancient black sewing machine, paste in new endpapers, and reinforce cracked spines. Sometimes I pawed through the box of discarded books that were deemed beyond repair and was allowed to bring some of them home.

I loved everything about the library, except the work. Shelving piles of books, hour after hour, with nothing to show at the end of the day except more piles of books was what I considered to be circular work; at quitting time, everything looked exactly as it had when I'd started. Yes, I had put away a thousand books (or so it felt), but people had also returned another thousand, and there they sat, waiting for me, the piles looking just like the piles I'd faced when I'd arrived. There was nothing tangible, nothing that I could bring home and say, "This is what I did today!" no real evidence that I had been at work at all. Time didn't crawl in that job. It didn't even stop. I swear it went backward; I would look at the clock and think, *Damn, I was sure it was past four, and here it is, only a quarter to three.*

My boss, Mrs. Hyvarinen, had twice gone to the library director, trying to get me a raise, but in five years she succeeded in bumping me up by only twenty cents an hour. This did not make much of a difference, and by the time I got to college I needed something more. I was thinking quite conventionally—maybe I could be a receptionist or a secretary. I had seen the ads in the paper—secretarial jobs paid $500 a month. It seemed a fortune. My mother, meanwhile, had high hopes that I would become a flight attendant, so that she and the rest of my beloved and gigantic family could fly around the world for free. But I could not picture myself serving people coffee while wearing a jaunty navy blue hat. I especially could not picture myself serving *my family* coffee while they were flying off somewhere fabulous for free and I was stuck on an airplane. Mrs. H. was my salvation. "You like to write. Maybe you could get a job at the newspaper, or one of the TV stations," she said.

I was briefly dazzled: Hmmmmm . . . television!

The local papers were looking for a newsroom clerk, someone to answer the city desk phone, write obituaries, and compile the marriages, divorces, bankruptcies, and other matters of record. It sounded like great fun. The newspaper offices were in a two-story brick building on West First Street, conveniently across the street from the Civic Center—quick access to the courthouse, the jail, the police station, the federal building, the county commissioners' offices, and the mayor. Even more convenient, I realized some time later, was its quick access to a bar (the Chinese Lantern) and another bar (the Pioneer). Two newspapers were published each day—the morning *News-Tribune*, and the evening *Herald*. The *Herald* staff came in at four thirty or five in the morning, and the paper came up off the press around noon and was delivered to homes in time for dinner. The *News-Tribune* was published twelve hours later, at around midnight, and landed on doorsteps in time for breakfast.

The newsroom was on the second floor—one big room crammed with battered metal desks, each equipped with a beige electric typewriter and a red telephone. The dayside *Herald* reporters shared desks, phones, and typewriters with the *News-Tribune* nightsiders; during the overlap in the middle of the day, the room was crowded. From the minute I walked in the door, I was entranced. I loved the noise and clutter and busyness—the clattering typewriters, the squawking, staticky police radio, the ringing telephones, the steady clickety-clacketing newswire machine. Every now and then a copy editor walked over and ripped a long furl of news right off the wire and carried it back to the horseshoe-shaped copy desk, folding up the pale yellow paper as he walked. Reporters—mostly middle-aged white men with paunches and balding heads—typed furiously, heads tilted at a painful angle, phones cradled between ear and shoulder in a position I came to think of as the Journalist Hunch. A blue haze of cigarette smoke hung in the air, punctuated by the rich smell of percolating coffee.

From where I stood, shyly waiting to talk to the managing editor, I could see a long strip of cardboard dangling from the wall with phone numbers inked by hand: Superior cops, Duluth fire department, St. Louis County sheriff, tugboats. Another strip of cardboard translated the police codes that constantly crackled across the scanner. They, too, were in huge type, readable from across the room, and the important ones were in red: 10-52, accident with injuries; and 10-54, death. All around me, men barked into phones, hollered back and forth, hustled to and fro carrying wire copy, news releases, photographs, cameras, notebooks, and coffee mugs. I had lived in Duluth all my life but had never known there was such a vibrant place as this.

The job of newsroom clerk was a new position, meant to relieve some of the drudgery of the reporters. Drudgery, I figured, was in the eye of the beholder. You don't know drudgery until you've shelved library books for hours every day, and then, when they're finally all put away, stood for additional hours reading the shelves, book by book, to make sure they were in the proper order. Now that's drudgery. Nothing in a newsroom could compare to that, I was sure. The newsroom clerk would work for both papers, coming in around nine in the morning and going home around six. And the pay! My god! An astounding $120 a week. And if you got sick, they paid you anyway. And if you needed to take a vacation day or two, they still paid you. And twice a day, every day, stacks of newspapers, still warm from the press, the ink smudging off on your hands, every word written just hours before. This was the job for me. I had interviewed at one of the TV stations too, but the hell with them. Print was my destiny; I was sure of it. I met with the managing editor, I took a typing test and blew everyone away with my 140 words per minute, I shook hands with a whole bunch of quivery old men, some of them in suspenders, many of them smoking.

And then I didn't get the job.

Tom Daly, the managing editor, called to tell me. He said the right things—I was great, they were impressed—but they had hired someone else, who was apparently just a tad more impressive in all regards. I slunk back to my ninety-five-cent-an-hour library job, crushed and demoralized. At noon, I walked outside and hid behind the hedge and wept, just a little.

A week later, Tom Daly called again. The new clerk had already quit. Did I still want the job? I didn't even stop to wonder what possibly hellish circumstances might have chased the clerk out in a mere five days. I just thrilled at my good luck. It took me about sixteen seconds to give notice, walk six blocks down the street, and start my new life.

·

Not Making Coffee

FRITZ NOTHACKER HAD ALREADY BEEN AT WORK FOR
four hours when I climbed the stairs to the newsroom on
Monday morning at the dot of nine. May 11, 1976, was my
first day on the job as newsroom clerk. My stomach was flut-
tering, so I skipped breakfast and left my half-eaten bowl
of cereal in the sink. I twisted my frizzy hair into braids,
pinned them across my head, and boarded the bus for the
ride downtown to the newspaper office, where I had been
told to report to Fritz. He was the city editor of the afternoon paper, the *Herald*. He had dark curly hair and looked
so much like my junior high school science teacher that I
had trouble calling him by his first name; I wanted to call
him Mr. Nothacker. But there are no Misters in a newsroom.
Most people went by their last names, shouted out over the
din: "Karlstrand! Cohen! Ormandy!" Fritz answered the
phone with a barking "City desk, Nothacker!" that unnerved
and impressed me. Later, when I picked up the phone, I
could only manage a timid, "City desk, Laurie." Much as I
wanted to call myself Hertzel, brusquely, I just didn't have
it in me.

Fritz sat at the city desk, which was just two ordinary
desks pushed face-to-face with a tall Rubbermaid trash can

in between. All day long, he sifted through mail and press releases and wire copy, tossing the wadded-up rejects into the trash without looking up. By the end of the day, the trash can was full, and balls of paper were scattered around him on the floor. The copy desk was off to his left; the rows of desks where the reporters sat were off to his right. The city desk was in the middle of it all, the heart of the newsroom. This is where I, too, would sit, opposite Fritz, until Jack Tyllia, the night city editor, came in at three and I had to relinquish his desk.

My tour that first morning started with the glassed-in editorial office, where Archie Salyards worked. Archie was tall, balding, and courtly, a Yale-educated writer who had a wall full of awards. People told me that he could have worked at any newspaper in the country but chose to stay in Duluth. That made sense to me. I couldn't imagine going anywhere else, either. Fritz explained the invisible wall between the newsroom and the opinion pages—how neither was allowed to influence the other; how no one in the newsroom had any say in what editorial writers wrote, and how none of the editorial writers could consult with reporters except on points of fact. He took me through the executive offices of the publisher, a tall, rangy white-haired guy from Albuquerque with a southwestern twang and cowboy boots. He had sharp eyes and a lazy way of asking sharp questions. Most publishers come up through the ranks of advertising, but John McMillion was an old news guy, and he liked to hang out in the newsroom, perched on the edge of someone's desk, chatting with reporters and floating story ideas. For years, he tried to get someone interested in writing about how the American Southwest might someday build a pipeline to drain away the water from Lake Superior, but as I recall the reporters shrugged every time he brought it up. It sounded, at the time, utterly implausible.

McMillion had a very stiff and proper general manager, a guy who looked like a character right out of a 1940s movie—dark suits, a fedora, and a thin mustache. Every morning before he arrived, his secretary was required to remove his typewriter cover, fold it, and place it in his bottom desk drawer. The general manager had been known to complain that coming in and finding the typewriter still covered was enough to set his whole day in the wrong direction. The secretary, when she told me this, did not look as if this worried her very much. I instantly liked the secretaries, and I saw myself as one of them—the support staff that watched the show with interest and amusement. It had not yet occurred to me that I could be part of the show.

The newsroom was almost entirely male; you could count the women on two hands, even if you were missing a couple of fingers. There were two young kick-ass women reporters—Jacqui Bananas and Suzanne Perry. There was a tough old bird named Janet Burns, who had been the city editor for a stint and was now reporting again. She wore dark blue suits and had thinning gold hair, and she was so no-nonsense that I was afraid of her. She wore hats. There was a librarian, and a chunky, fast-walking copy girl, and the two women who put out the "women's section"—Julie and Effie, who were sequestered in a remote office down a hallway next to the employees-only stairs.

But that was it. Everyone else in the room was male—the editor, the managing editor, the assistant managing editor, both of the city editors, all of the copy editors, most of the reporters, the entire sports department, all the photographers, and all of the printers (except for Millie, who was scary and deaf). Some wore suspenders. Some wore hats at their desks. Many of them smoked. One redheaded guy had beefy Popeye arms with tattoos; his beat was the Duluth harbor and the longshoremen, and every year he took off the entire month of November to go work on the docks. His pica pole—those metal rulers that measure off inches on one side, newspaper picas on the other—was engraved with his name, Richard L. Pomeroy, and the slogan "I cover the waterfront."

Fritz took me downstairs to the pressroom, where I saw huge thrumming machinery and men in leather aprons, plastic ear protectors, and small, square hats folded out of newsprint. The presses ran most of the time, Fritz explained, because when they weren't printing the two daily papers, they were printing Sunday inserts and advance sections. Then he took me back up to the newsroom, and I learned my duties. Answering phones, writing obituaries, compiling the marine log, walking across the street and collecting matters of record from the courthouse—all that sounded great. What did not sound great was this: making coffee.

The room lived on coffee. The men drank it by the gallon, all day and into the night, and it was up to me to make sure that the big urn in the corner never ran dry. I might have been timid, but I had a strong sense of fairness. I didn't drink coffee, so I saw no good reason why making it should be my responsibility. Also, it was logistically complicated. The only place with a sink deep enough to hold the coffee urn was the men's bathroom. There was a women's restroom on our floor, but it was a tiny, one-hole affair with a shallow sink, located directly across from the sports department. This meant that every time one of the seven women on the floor had to pee, the sportswriters didn't just know it, they could hear it. It was a humiliating bathroom for a shy person, and it was of absolutely no use in making coffee.

To make coffee I had to lug the urn down the hall to the men's room, pound on the door, yell, "Is anybody in there?" and then go in and fill it up at the big, deep sink, hoping that no guy came in needing to take a whiz, and then stagger with it back down the hall, water sloshing my ankles. This was not something I was inclined to do, so I set about scheming to get out of this responsibility. First, I started bugging guys when they were at their busiest. "Can you fill the coffeepot for me? There's someone in the bathroom." They didn't care to be interrupted when they were on deadline, and they didn't want to be away from their phones when they were waiting for a call back from a source, so this drove them a little nuts. And then I made coffee . . . badly. Undrinkably so. In a newsroom, that's saying a lot. Guys sauntered over to the coffeepot, filled their blackened cups, took a deep swig, and then coughed and choked. Maybe they even spat it out onto the linoleum floor. "GAAAA! Who made this?" And someone would give a nod in my direction. I was over at the city desk, answering the phone and typing obituaries and throwing wadded-up press releases into the trash without looking—you know, trying to appear swamped and important, just like Fritz—and I said, "Isn't it any good? Sorry. I don't drink coffee. I don't know how it's supposed to taste."

So it wasn't too long before that responsibility just sort of evaporated, and I could concentrate on the fun stuff:

snooping around the county courthouse among the bankruptcies, marriage license applications, and divorces, calling the fire chief to get the fire runs ("food on stove" was
a common one, as was "dryer fire," which almost certainly
launched my lifelong paranoia about leaving the dryer
going when I'm not home), and writing short, newsy items
for our daily "Duluth Briefs" roundup. When the *Herald*
came up off the press in the early afternoon and was delivered to each desk by Nancy, the copy girl, I opened it up,
turned to the Duluth Briefs, and stared at them with love.

I wrote that. I wrote that. I read them over and over. I got
no byline, no tagline—most of them were written straight
off of news releases and required no human contact whatso-
ever. But even so, there was something magical about seeing words that I had written put into print and distributed
for all the world to read.

Those were not my only duties. I also called down to the
harbor twice each day to get the information for the marine
log: the names of the big cargo ships that had passed under
the Aerial Bridge or through the locks at Sault Ste. Marie,
headed to and from the Duluth harbor. I learned to call them
ore boats, not ships, and to distinguish a laker (one that
traveled the Great Lakes) from a saltie (one that crossed
the ocean). The lakers made short trips to Thunder Bay and
Toledo and Cleveland and came through often, and their
names quickly became familiar to me—the *Arthur Anderson,* the *Cason J. Callaway,* the *William Irvin.* Accuracy was
paramount. "You don't want to get this wrong," one of the
old-time editors told me, a guy named Alex who everyone
called, for some reason, Bob. "Make sure you don't miss a
boat, or say it's outbound when it's inbound." Women—the

wives and girlfriends of the sailors—study the marine log to learn when to expect their man's boat back at port, he said. It gives them time to get their boyfriends out of the house. He told me that more than one angry woman had called the newsroom, demanding to know why we hadn't warned her that her husband's boat was headed home.

I believed his story, as I believed all the stories the old guys told me. The paunchy old guys became my friends. They yelled into their phones and smoked one cigarette after another and sometimes hollered at Fritz or Jack, and one of them, I found out later, kept an extensive collection of pornography in his desk drawer. But to me they were grandfatherly and kind, and they went out of their way to be helpful. Les Ormandy, the business editor, who had a luxurious swoop of white hair and a ratty beige raincoat that he wore winter and summer, brought me boxes of books that he and his wife were winnowing from their collection. Bob Hull, the jittery religion writer who wore loud plaid pants with a wide white vinyl belt and once dropped his false teeth on the floor, explained the ins and outs of newsroom protocol to me. Karl Jaros, the chief photographer, who was born in Bosnia and spent time in a German prison during World War II, listened to my baffled questions about the room and gave sage advice. He had made his way to America with his life savings hidden inside an accordion, and his war experiences had not made him bitter but had made him extremely kind. I talked to them more than I talked to the young women reporters, who seemed worlds away from me in sophistication and experience. Jacqui and Suzanne and, within a few months, new hires Ruth Hammond and Sue Willoughby, were so *busy*. They were confident and energetic. They chatted and laughed at things that I barely understood. They were like glamorous older sisters: there to admire and learn from but not necessarily to hang around with.

Jacqui Bananas—real name, Banaszynski—was tall and dark-haired and supremely self-confident. When she came back from assignment, she held the newsroom enthralled with her hilarious stories about the people she had interviewed that afternoon; she had a great eye for quirky detail, and a ready, generous laugh. She would toss her notebook and car keys onto her desk and start talking—maybe just to Suzanne or Willoughby, but the whole room would get quiet, and everyone would listen, especially me. Her beat was St. Louis County and later was expanded to include the region that stretched from Grand Rapids in northern Minnesota to Upper Michigan, from Willow River south of Duluth to the Canadian border, that whole vast area we called the Northland. I watched from behind my typewriter as she swooped into the office, grabbed a set of staff-car keys from the little wooden box under the police scanner, and took off for points north, sometimes for days at a time. Grand Marais, International Falls, places I had been with my family on day trips but not places where I had considered that lives of great drama might be played out, or news might be happening. But she always came back with stories, and they ran in the paper, often on the front page.

One of them was the story of Harmon Seaver, who was arrested that July for firing a rifle at a U.S. Forest Service helicopter. Seaver and his family lived in a log cabin down what Jacqui called a "dusty and time-rattled" road deep in the forests of Cook County in northern Minnesota. He logged, and his wife worked part-time as a nurse, but mostly they lived off the land. They had no electricity, no indoor plumbing; they grew their own food, tended livestock, and collected water from a creek. The helicopter regularly came by, spraying the herbicide 2,4-D on Forest Service land to kill the ground cover and help seedling pines grow. But Seaver objected. He worried that the chemicals were dangerous and were contaminating the creek that his family depended on for drinking water, and he demanded that the spraying be stopped. The Forest Service not only refused to stop spraying but said it would be impossible to notify him when they might spray again. It maintained that the herbicides were perfectly safe.

So the next time one of the helicopters whirled overhead, Seaver fired away. One shot, straight up through the treetops—a blank, he said. He was arrested by Cook County deputies, who surrounded his log cabin with guns drawn. "I don't want to go to jail for this," Seaver told Jacqui. "But I'm willing to go to jail to stop them from spraying. That's worth it."

It didn't occur to me then that the Seaver story was a bellwether, an early glimpse of a new concern for the environment, of organic farming, of citizens challenging the government on land rights. I just thought it was a great story about a colorful guy. I started reading the paper a little more closely, looking for these tales. That was the kind of story that I liked, and I pushed through the underbrush of everything else to find them.

It was a fortunate time to be working at a newspaper. You can see, looking back, that we were on the cusp of many issues that were about to burst open and influence the news for decades. In Wisconsin, Native American students were walking out of class, protesting the way the white teachers treated them and their traditions. Their parents were beginning to exert hundred-year-old treaty rights to spearfish and hunt, and they were met with strong resistance and bitter protest. In northern Minnesota, folks were growing increasingly angry at what they saw as the government meddling in their lives: People who had been hunting and fishing and snowmobiling all their lives were furious that moves were under way to make the Boundary Waters Canoe Area a no-motors area, and farmers were angry about the federal government's move to protect eastern timber wolves, which they believed were killing their chickens and cattle. In protest, severed wolf heads began showing up at courthouses and other public buildings all over the northern half of the state. A wolf head was left at the *News-Tribune* too, in a large cardboard carton on the secluded employees-only stairwell. Jacqui came back from assignment late one night, found the box, carried it up into the newsroom, and opened it. After that, the company installed a security system, and you could no longer get into the building after hours without swiping a magnetic card.

When I was young, my parents subscribed to three newspapers—the *Duluth Herald*, the *Duluth News-Tribune*, and the *Courier-Journal* from Louisville, Kentucky, where I was born. The *Courier-Journal* arrived several days late, in the mail, and I loved it because it had two full pages of comics. I grew up reading the funnies and Dear Abby, graduated to the editorial page and its lively letters to the editor, and eventually found my way to the news. But traditional news had always struck me as a dull, dutiful read, which is why tales like Harmon Seaver's were so delightful. It became clear to me that at the *Duluth News-Tribune*, the news was starting to change—the way it was defined, and the way it was written—largely because of Jacqui, Suzanne, Ruth, and Willoughby. It was becoming more human, more personal. Reporters still droned on importantly about city council meetings and legislative hearings and zoning board agendas, but by 1976 they were also starting to explore social issues in a way that I had not noticed before. Suzanne Perry went undercover at a local massage parlor and wrote about what it was like. She didn't find out anything terribly scandalous, and it was clear the other masseuses didn't quite trust her—"Who are you again?" they asked. "A college student?"—but her story made the front page nonetheless. Enlightening enough, perhaps, just to let readers know that these places existed, and to hear the voices of the women who worked there. Ruth Hammond interviewed the down-and-out people who lived in a string of small, shabby houses underneath the soaring Blatnik Bridge in Superior. One of the women told her that she could never move away because the spirit of her dead mother still lived in the house. Sometimes she heard it knocking on the walls.

It was a series of stories by Sue Willoughby, though, that impressed me the most. Sue was short and strong, with rough wavy hair. She smoked. She swore. She had a great, loud laugh. She was also observant, and she knew a good story when she saw one. She wrote about the lives of the indigent old men who lived in rented rooms along First Street, not far from the newspaper office. I had seen those old guys all my life, hanging around on corners and smoking their cigarettes in doorways, whenever I walked down

First Street on my way to Fichtner's Butcher Shop or the
European Bakery. I had never even given them a second
glance. Living in Duluth, it was understood that Superior
Street was where the nice shops were, and First Street was
where the trade shops and divey bars were and where the
bums hung out, especially down by the Union Gospel Mission. I had not questioned this, had not looked at the situa-
tion with any curiosity. And I had certainly never talked to
any of these men.

But Sue had. She got to know them—who they were,
and why they lived there, and what their lives had been
like years before. She climbed the stairs to their stuffy little
rooms and poked around in the dim, beery First Street bars
where they hung out, and she wrote their stories for the
newspaper. I wasn't used to stories like this, stories about
real people who don't normally get interviewed, stories
about people I saw in my day-to-day life but knew nothing
about. This, to me, was more compelling than a thousand
county board stories or reports on tonnage at the Duluth
harbor.

I like this, I remember thinking. *This is the kind of story
I would like to write someday.* But that wasn't yet a dream; it
was barely even a passing thought. I still thought I wanted
to write fiction someday, not journalism. And there was
such a gap between me and those young women—they had
graduated from college and had moved here from other
places, while I was just a year out of high school and still
plugging away at college at night. They checked out staff
cars and drove all over the Arrowhead, and I was still ped-
aling my orange ten-speed everywhere or taking the bus.
It was my shameful secret that, completely cowed by the

gory true-life car crash movie *Signal 30* that all junior high students had to watch before being allowed to take driver's ed, I had not even tried to get a driver's license. And, most important, Jacqui and Ruth knew how to chat with strangers, and I was still much more comfortable standing on the sidelines, watching. I did not know then how crucial those powers of observation are for a writer, or how useful they would eventually prove.

Jacqui, Suzanne, Sue, and Ruth began changing the newsroom and the news coverage in dramatic ways. It did not feel like a revolution at the time; it felt like evolution. It just felt like life unfolding. But it has been described to me since as a revolution, and I can see how it might have felt that way to those paunchy men in their fedoras and suspenders. The men in the room were far from outnumbered, but they had to learn to cope with this influx of bright young women. That included me, in my prim pinned-up braids and long corduroy skirts. Every morning I took my place across from Fritz, opened the mail, and answered the phone. In the afternoon, when Jack showed up, I moved to whatever available desk I could find. As reporters wandered in, claiming their turf, I bounced from desk to desk to desk. I didn't much care where I sat, in general, but I did not like the desk that belonged to reporter C. D. Schmidt. His typewriter had a short cord, and every few minutes I would bump it with my foot and have to crawl under the desk to plug it in. One afternoon I started to crawl back out when I saw a pair of cowboy boots blocking my way. They belonged to an editor, who was standing in front of me, his legs spread in a manly way, his thumbs hooked in the belt loops of his corduroy jeans, his index fingers pointing straight down. I looked up, but I did not look all the way up. I saw only boots, jeans, fingers, thumbs, and then I dropped my eyes again. I heard him snicker. And then I heard him speak. "There's something about the sight of a woman on the floor . . ." His voice trailed away as the copy desk burst out laughing.

My face flushed with embarrassment. I was not entirely sure what he meant, though I had a pretty good idea. I managed to get out from under the desk by crawling around him—not very dignified but better than going between his legs, which was the only other route. I brushed off my knees and sat down at the typewriter without a word. And as I tried to concentrate on the marine log, I got madder and madder. I argued with myself: I knew I should stand up for myself, say something, file a complaint. But the truth was, I didn't want to; I didn't like to make a fuss. I knew he meant it as a joke, and I didn't want to look like I couldn't handle it. But I couldn't stop thinking about it, and I didn't calm down, and so finally I screwed up my courage and walked into the office of the assistant managing editor, Bob Knaus. Even as I headed toward his open door, I hoped he was gone. The best of both worlds—the courage to complain without ever having to utter a word! But Bob was sitting at his desk, and he looked up when I walked in.

I wasn't sure how best to do this, so I told him, without preamble, and with many hmmms and ummms, that I wanted an apology. Knaus looked surprised, and his answer didn't help. "What for?" he said.

I tried to tell him (more hmmms and ummms), but he said only, "Yeah, I saw that. I thought it was funny." Apparently he couldn't see that I was quaking in fear and anger and embarrassment. Or maybe he could; I was not one to stand up for myself. I was not anything like Jacqui or Suzanne, who pointed out inequities practically every day. Finally Knaus said, "If you think you need an apology, I'll talk to him." I walked back to Schmidt's desk, pondering that. Did I think I needed an apology? Or did I deserve an apology? Or was I making a big prudish fuss over a harmless newsroom joke?

The next day, the cowboy-booted editor came up to me. He looked at the ground, he looked past my face, he looked everywhere except directly at me. He fumbled with an unlit cigarette. He said, "I'm not sure what I did that offended you, but whatever it was, if I upset you, I'm sorry." It wasn't a gracious apology; I wasn't even sure it was an honest apology, and his giving it embarrassed us both. Neither of us looked the other in the eye. But it would have to do. Bit by bit, the presence of young women in the room was bringing about some change.

·

Eyewitness to Change

··

YOU COULDN'T SEE LAKE SUPERIOR FROM MY PARENTS'
front porch. The view was obscured by the tall brick church
across the street and by the smudge of treetops just beyond,
which we grandly called the Allens' Woods. (It was really
just part of our neighbors' yard.) But six blocks straight
down the hill, there it was, deep blue, screaming with
seagulls, glittering in the sun; or gunmetal gray, choppy
and dotted with whitecaps; or no color at all, brightening to
a band of intense white at the horizon. It dominated everything, from the weather to directions: East, West, Over the
Hill, and By the Lake, which was always colder.

We lived East, on Fourth Street, in a gray house with a
red front step. Tall elm trees lined our street, forming a leafy
canopy overhead. The ten of us Hertzel kids grew up playing Red Rover in the churchyard, stealing apples from Mr.
Hammer's trees, sledding down the church hill, one big family in a neighborhood of big families. One stormy night, my
older brother Paul tucked the microphone of his reel-to-reel
tape recorder up against the screen of his bedroom window
and recorded a storm—the drumming rain, the crashing
thunder, the two-note moaning of the foghorn. In those
days, when I was younger and still living at home, Duluth

was a vibrant, working city of 106,000 people, the third-largest in the state. It was divided neatly in half—blue-collar West, white-collar East, with downtown in the middle. In West Duluth, Clyde Iron and U.S. Steel had jobs enough for anyone who wanted them—good jobs, even for boys fresh out of high school. They could graduate from Denfeld High one day and walk down to the steel plant the next and get a job that would take care of them for the rest of their lives. Or they could work on the boats; some of the East End boys I went to school with talked about getting jobs on the lakers, even though they knew that union cards were hard to come by. April through November, the harbor was busy with boats loading up coal and taconite and Dakota wheat and then gliding back out into the lake toward eastern ports—Detroit! Thunder Bay! Cleveland!—and adventure. And there was always talk about the possibility, some day, of year-round shipping. Our neighborhood was white-collar; my friends' fathers were bankers and merchants and, like mine, university professors. My brothers found after-school jobs easily, making egg rolls at Jeno's Pizza factory and washing dishes at Joe Huie's café down on Lake Avenue, a place my mother considered seedy. She said it was for sailors.

By 1976, when I started working at the paper, the boom times were over. Factories were shutting down, and people were moving away, mainly to the Twin Cities, following the jobs. The census for 1970 had been panicky, with officials determined not to lose first-class city status—and its money and prestige—by falling below 100,000. Even worse, they worried about being surpassed in size by fast-growing Bloomington, just outside of Minneapolis. We all hated Bloomington, even though we had never been there. We didn't consider it a real city, just a suburb. Who did they think they were, trying to depose us? My mother told me that Duluth census takers that year were urged to count every last person—even the sailors who had come into port. Somehow, they were successful; when the new numbers came out, Duluth squeaked past 100,000 with 500 to spare, but that was the last time. U.S. Steel closed, first the blast furnaces of the hot side, then the finishing mills of the cold side, ending thousands of jobs. Five years later, Universal Atlas Cement shut down. The cement plant's towering smokestack loomed for a few more years over the border of Morgan Park and Gary-New Duluth, but was quiet now, no longer showering the neighborhoods with smoke and ash. Residents were happy the soot was gone, but its absence was a reminder of livelihoods lost.

By then I had boldly moved a full mile away from home to a neighborhood that we called the Reporters' Ghetto—shabby old mansions in the near East End that had been carved up into rental rooms and apartments. I rented two furnished rooms on the second floor of a big house on Sixteenth Avenue East and Superior Street. The refrigerator and sink were in the bedroom, and a small greasy stove squatted in a corner of the sitting room. You had to light the burners with a match, and so I never did. I lived on cereal and cold sandwiches, and threw away my dirty dishes instead of washing them. (I bought a new supply, regularly, at Goodwill for a dime apiece.) The bathroom was down the hall and shared, but I had grown up in a house with eleven other people and was used to that. A lonely, chatty woman lived at the top of the stairs. Every night when I came home I tiptoed up to the second floor, trying to put no weight on the squeaky tread, and every night I would make it almost to the top and her door would fly open and she would talk and talk and talk.

In the morning, I caught the bus downtown to the *News-Tribune*. Or if the weather was nice and I was up in time, I walked. My route took me along Superior Street, the lake glittering to my left. I walked past the Kitchi Gammi Club, which banned women (except as guests of men, and even then they had to use the side door); the mammoth, echoing Sears store on the edge of downtown, where my mother, and other mothers, shopped less and less often now that the Miller Hill Mall had opened on the edge of town; and a whole lot of empty storefronts. I walked one steep block up the hill to First Street, climbed the stairs to the second floor, and became part of the swirl of the newsroom. Duluth might have fallen on hard times, but it was a lively summer for news. We published two sections most days—news and sports—and they were packed with stories. Laying out pages wasn't yet called "designing" and wasn't yet seen as an art form, and stories were shoehorned in every which way on crowded and jumbled inside pages. Sometimes you found the interesting stuff almost by accident; it made me a careful reader because I didn't want to miss a thing.

Every day the front page carried some new twist in the plan to ban motors in the Boundary Waters Canoe Area, or news of another wildcat strike up on the Iron Range, or another point of drama in the Reserve Mining story. For years, the Silver Bay company had been dumping taconite tailings into Lake Superior, and now the lake water—our drinking water—tested high for asbestos. In July, a judge ordered Reserve Mining to shut down. Silver Bay residents were furious; Reserve was their main employer, really the only reason the town existed; and if the mine closed, almost everyone would end up out of work. Meanwhile, until they could figure out how to filter out the asbestos, Duluth city officials began giving away bottled water. But because the shutdown and the pollution were so controversial, it was seen as a political statement to accept the filtered water, and thousands of the plastic jugs piled up.

I watched the reporters with something like awe as they grilled sources, charged out of the room on their way to an assignment, and pounded out stories on deadline, and I was glad for my safe corner answering phones and taking obits. I could *never* do that job. We hired a few more women—our first female photographer, Joey McLeister, a quiet, slender woman with an unexpectedly wicked sense of humor, and a couple more reporters, Sandy Battin and Chris Paulson—but the room remained intensely male. Jokes flew at the women's expense, and in print women were still referred to by their husband's names. One of our copy editors liked to cut out the *Lockhorns* cartoon and paste it up at his desk; the shrewish Loretta Lockhorn, he said, was just like his wife. When a woman in the newsroom got married, one of the old-timers asked her gravely if she planned to quit her job.

I had a healthy respect for authority, and in my eyes the other women were fearless. One afternoon when the little one-hole women's bathroom across from the sports department was occupied, Suzanne Perry walked boldly into the men's room. When another reporter arranged to meet a source at the Kitchi Gammi Club and then was denied entrance at the front door, she came back to the office furious, kicking herself for obediently using the side

door. Bob Knaus liked to tease Jacqui and Suzanne about
their argumentativeness. When they grew particularly fervent, he asked if they were on the rag. Jacqui and Suzanne
responded by threatening to document their menstrual
cycles and present him with a "flow chart." That way, they
told him, you'll know if we're truly angry or just hormonal.

Answering the city desk phones and talking to readers,
I learned how deeply people cared about the *News-Tribune*.
They didn't just like the newspaper, they thought it belonged
to them. People called and wanted events publicized repeatedly; they wanted arrests left out of the "matter of record";
they wanted obituaries to be rerun adding shirttail relatives
and beloved pets as survivors. When I told them no, as I
often had to do, they grew frustrated. "But you're a public
service!" people told me more than once. No, we're a for-
profit business, I wanted to say, but didn't. I liked that they
cared so much, that they felt such ownership of the newspaper; it made me proud. But I knew who really had the power,
and in those years it wasn't the readers, and it wasn't the
advertisers.

One August afternoon, as I typed up yet another obit of
yet another long-lived Finn from the Iron Range (we used to
joke that every other obit was for a guy named Toivo Maki),
I watched Knaus walk out of his office and head to the bulletin board. He tacked up two sheets of pale green paper and
then walked back to his office without a word. A little knot
of reporters gathered. One editor shook his head slowly and
then walked away muttering, "This is stupid. This is really
stupid." I waited until the knot had dispersed, and then I
slipped over to take a look.

The memo was unsigned. NEWS-TRIBUNE AND HER-

ALD POLICY ON TREATMENT OF WOMEN IN NEWS COL-
UMNS, the headline said. THIS POLICY WILL COVER ALL
SECTIONS OF BOTH NEWSPAPERS.

No longer would women be referred to by their husband's names (a long-standing gripe of my mother's). No
longer would they be referred to as girls or grandmothers
or coeds. Their physical appearance would no longer be
part of the story, unless it was somehow relevant—no more
pretty, petite, spry, or blonde. Job titles would become gen-
der neutral—no more spokesman or spokeswoman, no more
councilman or councilwoman. Chairman and chairwoman
would become, simply, "chair." (This led, a few years later,
to a memorable caption under a society section photo of the
Junior League, written by an editor with a sense of humor.
In the picture, each woman was identified by her committee
assignment—and so you had, from left to right, the Fund-
Raising Chair, the Refreshments Chair, and the Dining
Room Chair.) The memo also stated that we were abolish-
ing courtesy titles. No more Mrs. Anderson, just Anderson.
Eight months before, the paper had run a Page One story
about Elnora Johnson, the first woman to be elected president of the city council. The first paragraph, the lede, read,
"For the first time ever, a Duluth City Council president's
first unofficial act Monday evening was to put on her lipstick." Under the new policy, that kind of lede would no longer fly.

The room was abuzz, and not everyone was happy. The
change had been spearheaded by Jacqui and Suzanne,
who had pushed it with top management. They had met
with Daly and Knaus for weeks, hashing out the details.
Would it be policy for all sections of the newspaper? Or

would the society pages be allowed to maintain the old standards? What about obits? What did other papers do? Is this too radical, or are we behind the times? Some of the other young reporters agreed with the change; they said it was overdue. But many of the old-timers hated it, and they responded with sarcasm and anger. You could hear heated discussions all over the newsroom, especially over those gender-neutral job titles; copy editors enjoyed pointing out how artificial it would be, and for a while some of them went to great lengths to put convoluted gender-neutral phrases in print. What are we supposed to call a fisherman? A fisher-person? (We went with "angler.") What about manhole covers? Huh? What do you call those? (Well, manhole covers, of course.)

That Sunday, a small box appeared on Page One alerting readers to the new style and guiding them to an awkward column written by the publisher. It was clear that John McMillion wasn't entirely sold on the policy; his column walked a fine line between respect and begrudgement, but I guess you had to give him credit for not standing in the way. "Since this is the last time I can call you females 'ladies' or 'girls' in these newspapers, I want to add this passing thought to the ladies and girls out there," he wrote. "You've come a long way, baby."

"If you are upset about some of these things, call Tom Daly," he added. "I'm chicken."

Letters poured in for weeks. The longer ones were usually the angriest. "Father was right: you're all nuts," one woman wrote. Another woman insisted that, as a "former frustrated feminist," she wanted to be referred to by her married name, Mrs. Roger Barton. She was sure that the newspaper would eventually be forced to overturn the new policy, at which time "we can return to the timeless beauty of the well balanced woman of Proverbs. She is all things the liberated woman tries to be, lacking the self-serving." It seemed a harsh critique of liberated women, to be accused of being self-serving merely for wanting to be called by their own names, and even though the letters continued, the new policy stood.

We kept a linotype machine in the lobby, as a reminder of the days of hot type, when compositors set each letter of each word by hand. Those days had ended a couple of years before I was hired. Now we typed our stories on scanner paper, using IBM Selectric typewriters equipped with a special square, sans-serif font that the computer could read and making a carbon copy for our records. Edits were written in by hand, with black felt-tipped pens, using the standard and time-honored copyediting marks. The job of the compositors was no longer to pick through lead letters or make zinc engravings of photos but to scan the stories into the computer, keyboard in the edits, and create half-tones from the photographs. Nancy, the copy girl, ran dummies, stories, and photos back and forth from the newsroom to the composing room. When she was on vacation, those duties fell to me, grabbing the sheaf of copy and darting down the hall past the sports department, turning left at the publisher's office, down a dark, narrow corridor, and then out into the bright and busy composing room, where men armed with X-Acto knives and hot wax pasted up the pages for the afternoon *Herald*.

The Associated Press stories still came in on a machine

that typed the stories, double-spaced, in all caps, on a roll of pale yellow paper. (And woe to anyone who let that machine run out of paper; the typing continued, keys clacking away on the bare platen.) Every so often the copy chief walked over and ripped off the latest news, read it, and decided what to publish. The stories that he didn't use were impaled on a sharp, thin metal spike by his desk. (And "to spike a story" still means to kill it.) I got accustomed to working in noise—the clattering typewriters and wire machine, the ringing phones, the muffled static of the police scanner. When the news was urgent, the wire machine rang a bell to get our attention. If it was a bulletin—president shot, war declared—the bell rang and rang and rang. Wire photos came in on another machine. They were large and slightly sticky and tended to fade over time to an unusable sepia. They were not permanent photos; they were news photos; here today, gone tomorrow, just like the newspaper itself.

This was a boom time for newspapers, and more change was on the way. Within the year, the company devised a faster way to get copy from the newsroom to the composing room. They installed pneumatic tubes through the ceiling, like at a drive-in bank. The copy desk supervisor, known as the slot, rolled up the copy and photos and stuffed them into the plastic cylinder. *Whoosh!* The tube was sucked up into the ceiling and spat out in the back shop within seconds. And that was it for Nancy. With no need for her to run copy, there was no need for her job, and she was let go. The rest of her duties, of course, fell to me—sorting the mail and bringing up stacks of *Heralds* off the press, and running down to the pressroom with last-minute changes from the copy desk while the press was still running. If a name had been spelled wrong or a headline had a typo, the pressmen could chisel the offending letter on the plate and so blur the error; this was why sometimes in your newspaper you saw a word that looked like it hadn't printed fully. That was how we fixed things on the run. I never yelled, "Stop the presses!" and I don't think anybody else ever did either—just handed the marked-up page to the head pressman. He wore ear protectors, anyway, and would not have heard me had I yelled.

I didn't think it was fair to give me Nancy's duties without increasing my pay. So I walked into Knaus's office and asked for a raise. This was not easy for me; I was painfully shy and still secretly thought it was kind of amazing that they paid me at all, but injustice was a powerful motivator.

Knaus just chuckled. "We'd all like a raise," he said.

·

Murder!

IT WAS MURDER THAT HOOKED ME ON NEWSPAPERS. The other news of the day—mayors and governors elected, laws passed, taconite plants shut down, barrels of Honeywell waste thrown into Lake Superior in the dead of night—all that was interesting enough. But it was the murders that grabbed me.

My first summer at the paper, a retired schoolteacher named Florence Hector disappeared. The prime suspect was her stockbroker, a man with movie-star good looks who had apparently embezzled $75,000 from her. He was already in trouble for stealing some valuable model trains from someone else. He also happened to be the father of two glamorous, intelligent girls I had known in high school, a fact that made the case particularly riveting. Miss Hector was never found, and no one was ever charged. The day the stockbroker was to appear in court on the model train charges, he jumped bail and wasn't seen again for months. Before disappearing, he told his family that he was being threatened by a guy in Toronto and was headed to Thunder Bay, but he was arrested about eight months later in Colorado while trying to sign on as a ranch hand. The whole thing was terribly sad and tragic for both families.

Still, "sad and tragic" would not be the words I would have used back then to describe the case. "Thrilling and exciting" would have been the words. And all the more exciting when I could talk to the reporter who was covering the story and get tidbits every morning that nobody else knew. (Jim Allen was convinced that he knew where Miss Hector's body was buried, and he kept trying to persuade the cops to dig up the stockbroker's new backyard patio.) I loved the way that stories like this unfolded over time, every day a new installment. Reading the newspaper was like reading a great novel, a chapter a day—except this great novel was true.

My second summer at the paper, David Berkowitz was arrested in the Son of Sam killings in New York City. I was curious. Oh, I was curious. I wanted to read every detail, everything I could find, which wasn't much. The news still came in on the Associated Press wire machine, typed rapidly onto that pale yellow copy paper, so I took to hanging around the copy desk and bugging the slot to let me read the latest developments. Alex Lyness, the *Herald* slot, would dig through the spiked stories and hand over early ledes to get me off his back.

But there was another murder that summer that was even more compelling: the Congdon murders. They were *ours*. They took place just a few miles from where I grew up, in a mansion overlooking Lake Superior along exclusive London Road.

Early on the morning of June 27, 1977, the call came crackling over the scanner: Possible homicide at Glensheen, the Congdon mansion. Two bodies had been discovered— Elisabeth Congdon, age eighty-three, dead. Her overnight nurse, Velma Pietila, dead. The day nurse had found them when she reported for work that morning. Fritz looked around the newsroom and grabbed whomever he had: he dispatched Sandy Battin, the education reporter, and photographer Karl Jaros. The *Herald* deadline was eleven thirty. They had three hours: *Go.*

Paul Brissett, who covered the state legislature, was heading to work along London Road when he saw cop cars parked in front of Glensheen, and Sandy and Karl, with notebooks and cameras, trudging down the driveway toward the mansion. When he got to work, he didn't even have time to ask what was going on before Fritz deployed him as the rewrite guy. When I got in a few minutes later, I was stunned by the electricity in the room. I had never felt such urgency in the air, never seen the old men move so fast. Over on the copy desk, Lyness was barking orders and clearing space on Page One. I was sent into the library— which was called the morgue—to pull clips and mug shots. I loved having a part of the action and wished I could do more; when I had finished my duties, I eavesdropped like mad so that I could find out the latest.

The Congdons were one of the most venerable families in town. I remembered them from years before, when I was in junior high school. Elisabeth's sister-in-law, Dorothy Congdon, who lived just a few doors down on London Road, had encountered an intruder who was trying to crawl in an upstairs window. She grabbed a shotgun and fired twice, hitting him in the groin, and the poor guy bled to death. He was only seventeen. And now this. Someone had broken a basement window of Glensheen, wriggled into the house, and headed up the stairs. Whoever it was had surprised the

night nurse on the staircase and bashed her over the head
with a candlestick. Miss Congdon was found dead in her
bed, a satin pillow over her face.

Elisabeth Congdon was the daughter of a mining mag-
nate named Chester Congdon, who had made a fortune on
the Iron Range. She lived in the family home, an imposing
brick mansion with diamond-paned windows and a wine
cellar and a jewel-green lawn that rushed down toward the
lake. She never married but had adopted two infant girls.
Like in a fairy tale, one was good, and one was not. The good
daughter, Jennifer Johnson, was beyond reproach, happily
married, a dutiful regular visitor to her mother. The other
daughter, Marjorie Caldwell, was trouble. She lived in Colorado; she and her husband, Roger, had constant financial
troubles. She was so mistrusted that she was not allowed to
see her mother without supervision. It wasn't long before
Marjorie's name came up in connection with the murders.
People were sure she must have had something to do with
this—perhaps prompted by a desire for the inheritance.
Sure enough, ten days later, Roger Caldwell was arrested.
Marjorie was eventually arrested as well, and in the end he
was convicted and she was not, but even now almost no one
believes the truth was that simple. The clues were too odd: a
gold coin stolen from the house, covered in Roger's finger-
prints and mailed from Duluth back to himself in Colorado.

After he had been imprisoned for five years, the state
supreme court ordered a new trial. A plea bargain, instead,
offered him freedom in exchange for a confession. Roger
Caldwell did confess, but he later recanted and eventually
committed suicide. Questions remain about who really
was in that house and who was behind the murders; it will

....

always be one of Duluth's great mysteries. Throughout my career at the *News-Tribune*, Marjorie Caldwell popped up in the news every few years, and always for extraordinary reasons. Arson. Attempted murder. Bigamy. Whenever you heard her name, you knew there was going to be another Page One story.

As exciting as it was to be part of the Congdon story in my own small way, I found it a challenge whenever they sent me into the morgue. It was nearly impossible to find anything back there. The library was a long, narrow L-shaped room just off the newsroom, tucked between the editorial page office and the wire room and lined with green metal filing cabinets. Each drawer was tightly stuffed with nine-by-fourteen-inch envelopes, which were crammed with clippings and photos and the occasional zinc. The dented drawers were crooked on their tracks, and sometimes you had to put a shoulder into it to get them shut.

Zincs were the reverse-engraved photos used during the days of hot type; they were thick and heavy, and the etched images were blue from ink. When you ran your finger over them, you could feel the lines scratched into the surface. Even though the paper had switched to cold type a few years before, the library files still held dozens of zincs, which meant that when you pulled an envelope, sometimes it was unexpectedly heavy, and it clunked.

Good luck to you finding anything in that place; the filing system was unfathomable. You were lost without the librarian, the only person who understood the arcane system under which every clipping was tucked away. But sometimes the system confounded even her, and she would stand in the back of the library and scratch her blonde head with a pencil.

Shirley Finberg was a tiny woman, barely five feet tall, and a former ballet dancer. Sometimes I would walk into the library and find her in the back among the cabinets, doing deep pliés to stay limber. She owned a whole wardrobe of identical polyester pantsuits in different colors—short-sleeved tops that buttoned up the front and cinched around the waist with a tie belt, and matching elastic-waist pants. Buttercup yellow, mint green, pale blue—a different pastel for every day of the week. She worked as a fitness coach for the University of Minnesota Duluth ski jumping team, teaching the athletes ballet exercises to help them stretch and soar. She believed in incorporating these moves into every aspect of life. And it's true, when Shirley had to pull a clip from a bottom drawer, she wouldn't squat or bend—once again, she would plié.

Shirley once told me that she kept the filing system convoluted quite deliberately—as long as editors couldn't find clips or photos without her help, her position at the paper was secure. But when she was well into her fifties, she remarried and quit, and they asked me if I wanted her job. I had filled in for her once or twice when she was on vacation, and I guess I understood that library as well as anyone. And I was getting a little tired of being a clerk, especially now that I had been given Nancy's responsibilities too. So I said OK and trudged back to the library, without stopping to think that I had fled the tedium of a library once before for the busyness and excitement of the newsroom.

My first day on the job one of the more sarcastic night-side copy editors taped a greeting to the library door: ABANDON HOPE, ALL YE WHO ENTER HERE.

My mandate was to overhaul the library and create a simple filing system that people could understand. Reporters and copy editors needed to find stuff quickly, on deadline, and the librarian wouldn't always be around to help. So much for perpetuating Shirley's vision of job security. It was not hard to figure out the logic behind her system, which was, basically, to think of the largest general category you could, and then subdivide, subdivide, subdivide. The hard part was thinking big enough to figure out that first category. That first category was key; without it, you were lost.

Some I already knew: clips about the local ski hill, Spirit Mountain, for instance, were filed under *G*, for government. And then the topic was subdivided repeatedly:

Government

City of Duluth

Businesses, city-owned

Ski hills

Mountain, Spirit

I also knew how to find the city council clips. They, too, were under *G*:

Government

City of Duluth

Council, City

As you can imagine, that *G* drawer was pretty crowded. But when Jack Shipley, our city hall reporter, came in looking for clips on UFOs, I was completely lost. I searched and searched and finally told him we didn't have any. It wasn't until months later that I happened across them. They were under *S*, for Saucers, Flying. If you could just train your mind to think backwards, you could find what you needed, but it was hard to do on deadline.

In the beginning, I had fun because they let me spend

money. I decided that I needed new file cabinets, with smaller drawers; instead of stuffing everything into those giant nine-by-fourteen white envelopes, I planned to have small envelopes just for the clippings, and file the photographs separately. So I made a list: I needed cartons of envelopes for the new files. The cabinets were tall, and so I needed a step stool. Time stood still back there (this should have been a warning to me), and I needed a clock. The stapler had vanished after Shirley left, so I needed a stapler.

The paper was in a buying mood; they bought me everything I asked for. (Note: This has never happened to me since.) All I had to do was fill out requisition slips and give a reason for each item. Reason for stapler: To staple. Reason for clock: To know the time. Reason for step stool: That one stumped me. Finally I wrote, "short librarian." Though truth be told I wasn't as short as the previous one.

After a few weeks, everything started arriving—sleek beige cabinets, rolled in on dollies; cartons of buff-colored envelopes; a sky blue step stool with black rubber wheels. Now I had to transform the place. I spent hours each day pulling out clips and recategorizing them, sliding them into clean new envelopes, and filing them in the nice new file cabinets with drawers that didn't stick. City council clips went under *C*, for city council. Spirit Mountain clips went under *S*, for Spirit Mountain. UFO clips went under *U*, for UFO. It felt bold and daring to type only one or two words on the outside of an envelope instead of lines of categories and subcategories, but that was about as bold and daring as library work was going to get. There were hundreds of files and thousands of clippings, and it would take a lot of time to recategorize everything, but there was nothing dif-

ficult about it in the least. It just took time. And as I soon
discovered, it wasn't very interesting work. I liked creating
the system. I did not like maintaining it.

Unfortunately, maintaining the files was the main part
of my job, the part that would go on and on long after the
reorganization was done. It was my job to physically cut
every local story out of each of the two daily papers with
a pair of deadly looking long-bladed shears and then file
them, sometimes in multiple places—under the reporter's
byline and under one or two or three topics. I also had to
collect the photos from the composing room and file those
as well. And then when reporters borrowed clips, they usually just tossed them in a metal basket on my desk when
they were done, and I had to put them away.

Zzzzzzzzzzzzzz.

Circular work. I was back to doing circular work.

That first day on the job, I went into the composing
room to pick up the photos that had run in that morning's
News-Tribune. It was the printers' job to scan the photos
into the computer and then toss them into a long cardboard
drawer each night, for the librarian to retrieve. I pulled open
the drawer, and there, on top of the photos, lay a pair of severed legs. Not human legs, of course, but the legs of some
kind of bird. A grouse, maybe, or a chicken. Tendons and
claws and all.

I stood there, and I looked at the legs, and I pondered
what to do. I knew I should cavalierly pick them up and say
something snappy, but I just didn't have it in me; despite
growing up in the hunting and fishing capital of the world,
I wasn't used to handling dead things. The printers were
watching me sideways, glancing away when I looked at

them. One of them finally met my eyes, and I took a step toward him. "Jim," I said, "could you move something for me?"

And Jim did. He picked up the legs and pulled the tendons. The clawed feet clenched. When I shuddered, the printers laughed.

The library became a sanctuary for unhappy reporters, who liked to get a cup of coffee, lean on my counter, and gripe. This kept me in better touch with the gossip than I had ever been before, but it didn't make up for the fact that I was now out of the newsroom. I could see everything from my desk by the doorway, but I was no longer part of the action. I no longer got to pick up a reporter's notebook, cross the street, climb the worn marble steps of the courthouse, and find out who was suing whom, or who was getting divorced (and why), or who was building a detached garage or adding a new front porch. No longer did I get to chat on the phone with the friendly young guy at the Corps of Engineers who flirted with me twice a day when I called for the shipping news, or yak with Charlie Bell of Bell Brothers, the most cheerful mortician in town, when he called with another Toivo Maki. I missed snooping.

I took to making up errands that got me out of the library. I would even have started making coffee again, if I had thought of it. As it was, I started drinking it, as an excuse to emerge back into the noisy room. And so I was hanging out in the newsroom one August afternoon when a strange woman walked up the stairs and paused at the top, by the editor's office. She was short and stocky with short dark hair, and that is all I can tell you about her appearance, because her eyes were covered by giant dark sunglasses and the lower half of her face was swathed in bloody bandages. She asked for Jim Allen, our cops reporter. She refused to give her name. She refused to say what she wanted. She refused to talk to anyone else. He was out doing rounds, someone told her.

"I'll wait," she said.

And she did, lurking at the edge of the room until Allen bounded up the stairs, his reporter's notebook in his back pocket. He took one look at her and stopped. Then he crossed the newsroom, whispered a few words to Jack Tyllia, grabbed a fresh notebook, and walked the woman down to the first-floor conference room.

I didn't see her again, but Jim had a front-page story the next morning: Marjorie Congdon Caldwell, daughter of the murdered heiress and one of the prime suspects in the crime, had been attacked. She told Allen that there had been a knock that morning on the door of her son's apartment in the Twin Cities suburb of Fridley, where she was staying. She said she had opened the door and a man in a uniform, waving a gun and a badge, slashed her with a razor. (Actually, the news stories, hedging so as to avoid a possible error, called the weapon "a razor-like instrument.") She said the man told her he would come back and do more damage to her and to her son if she tried to help her husband, Roger, beat the murder charge.

Nobody seemed to believe her story. The cops said it was nonsense. Still, she allowed Karl Jaros to photograph her bandaged and sunglassed face, and since that was the only mug shot we had of her, that picture, odd as it was, ran with every story we wrote about her for years.

I used to pop in now and then to chat with the two kind women who worked for what had once been called the society section. Reporter Effie Blubaugh was a friendly, jolly woman who was married to our outdoors writer, Jim. Her boss, Julie Agnew, was the editor of Today's Living, where you would find announcements of marriages and engagements, society news, recipes, and fashion. Julie had frosted blonde hair and was married to a young county attorney named Tom, and they had a whole bunch of sons. Five, I think. They seemed like the all-American East End family until Tom ran for city council. In his campaign ads, he looked handsome and paternal, with thick Glen Campbell hair and unfortunate plaid trousers, posing with his pretty wife and their smiling boys. This was exactly the kind of guy Duluthians wanted representing them, and he won the council seat handily.

But after Agnew took office in January, it became clear very quickly that something was wrong. It was hard to define, at first. Agnew had a passion for truth and ethics that seemed unique and admirable. He fought hard for the causes he believed in, and they were noble causes. He had no qualms about defending his beliefs, even when it meant fighting everyone else on the council, and the mayor, to boot. He had no interest in compromise. His first battle came right away, and it was a big one: City money that was supposed to be spent on low-income people somehow became earmarked for an over-the-freeway shopping center. The mayor and other councilors thought it a good idea and argued that it would help low-income people by boosting the economy and adding jobs. But Agnew opposed it. And when it passed the council, he filed a lawsuit to freeze the money.

For a brief time, he was hailed as a champion of the little guy. Everyone was talking about him, right from the get-go. The head of the Senior Coalition was his staunch supporter, even as other councilors and businessmen began backing away. But then Agnew filed another lawsuit. And another one. He began to file lawsuits with great frequency, almost as a matter of course, whenever someone took an action he opposed. He sued the council repeatedly, and sometimes he sued individual council members, stopping votes on all kinds of topics. He sued the mayor. When the newspaper ran one of Archie Salyards's editorials saying that Agnew had overstepped his bounds, he sued the newspaper. Over time, his behavior grew even more peculiar. He stopped showing up for key votes. He claimed illness and skipped council meetings, when people had seen him looking just fine earlier in the day. Within weeks of his taking office, people started talking recall. Six months into his term—the minimum amount of time determined by law—Thomas Gruesen, a local attorney, began circulating a recall petition. Gruesen had supported Agnew's campaign, but Tom's erratic behavior now caused him to turn against his long-time friend.

Agnew responded by calling a press conference to announce that he would file a defamation suit against anyone and everyone who signed the petition. Salyards wrote another editorial, supporting the recall. Agnew filed another lawsuit against the *News-Tribune*. He then sued to stop a judge from stepping down, and a week later, he entered the race for county attorney. It was all just so bizarre.

Such a crazy summer. Never had city council coverage been more riveting, the serial narrative of Agnew's breakdown unfolding a little more every morning in my paper.

At work, I devoured the stories of Agnew's zany behavior, even as I watched Julie grow anxious and thin. She was still uncertain whether her husband was principled beyond belief or slowly losing his marbles, and she defended him staunchly. Through it all the *News-Tribune* continued its exhaustive coverage, the handsome Glen Campbell campaign mug shot accompanying each story, though I wondered if Tom had gotten a little more disheveled and wild-eyed since that photo had been taken. In August, he initiated criminal action against himself, accusing himself of malfeasance for asking the mayor to fire the city assessor.

When a recall election was announced for that September, Julie decided to take action. She needed to show her husband support, but she also knew that voters might be reluctant to keep him in office, given his erratic behavior and the multitude of lawsuits. So she decided to run for his seat, to give voters an alternative.

Her plan was a perhaps noble but misguided gesture, and it cost her her job. The editor called her in the day after she filed and gave her the news. Journalists have no business running for office, he said. We cover politicians. We're watchdogs of the government. We can't be politicians too. Julie protested—she was the society editor, for god's sake. She had nothing to do with the paper's coverage of elections or politics or city government. But the editor was adamant. You can't run for office and also be an editor at a daily paper, he said. And Julie was fired.

In the end, Julie's entrance into the race split the vote—together she and Tom garnered a majority, but separately neither won enough votes to win, and Philip Sneve took the council seat. A few months later, a small news item appeared deep inside the *News-Tribune*: Tom Agnew had filed for divorce.

This was not the end of Agnew's public life; he continued to show up at council meetings and other civic events, usually carrying a picket sign. Just as he had been suing everyone left and right (including filing lawsuits on behalf of people who had not hired him nor wanted his help), he now began picketing events with just as much passion.

Archie Salyards had suffered from increasingly deep depression for several years, and in the summer of 1980 he died of suicide, a gunshot to the head. Agnew—never forgetting the editorials that Salyards had written about him—showed up at his funeral, standing outside of Holy Rosary Cathedral on East Fourth Street, holding a sign. "Guts but no brains," it said, in cruel reference to Salyards's manner of death, and Einar W. Karlstrand and Isadore Cohen, two of our old, paunchy, fedora-and-suspenders-wearing reporters, were so incensed they rushed him in fury and had to be restrained.

In my boredom, over time, when I should have been filing clippings, I got into the habit of circling typos and other errors in the paper and bringing them out to Bill Sniffen, the *News-Tribune* slot. I had no idea how obnoxious this was, and I didn't stop to think how frustrating it is to be shown your mistakes once they're in print and it's too late to do anything about them; I thought I was being helpful.

Sniffen was a sarcastic sort—it was he who had taped the "abandon hope" quote to my door—but he took my criticisms with grace. He also shrewdly figured he could put them to good use. "Do you want to work on the copy desk for the summer?" he asked. "Just to fill in, while people are on vacation?"

Did I? Did I? Now that sounded like the job for me—back in the newsroom, in the thick of things as they were happening instead of after they had happened, correcting copy, shooting stuff through the ceiling in pneumatic tubes, writing headlines, asking sharp questions of the reporters, *ordering around the newsroom clerk.*

By now, Knaus had been promoted to managing editor. He said a summer on the *Herald* desk was OK with him, as long as I didn't fall behind in my library work. In other words, as long as I could do two full-time jobs simultaneously and only get paid for the lower-paying job, no problem. I made a decision in a flash that he would never, ever know how far behind I fell in my filing. The summer on the copy desk was my door back into the newsroom, and I wasn't about to let the never-ending mountain of clippings stand in my way.

·

On the Night Desk

During my two years in the library, the news-paper had installed Atex computers at all the desks. This meant that, sadly, there was no more need for pneumatic tubes—all of the writing and editing were done on comput-ers, and copy editors sent stories to the composing room electronically. (They still trotted the page dummies and photos back by hand.) The Associated Press stories came in on the computer as well, and the clacketing wire machine was no more. The newsroom was getting to be a quieter place—just the clicks of computer keys and the occasional hissing squawk from the police radio.

The copy desk, in those days, was a modified version of the traditional U-shaped desk. The slot sat in the dip of the U, and the rimmers sat on either side, along the rim. The slot's job was to run the desk, lay out pages, including Page One, and order up headlines and trims. The ads had been marked earlier in the day, and the slot had to take note not only of their location but also of their content, so as to avoid unpleasant juxtapositions—no cigarette ads on the obits page, for instance, and no Republic Airlines ad on the same page as a news story about an airplane crash. It was the job of the rimmers (known at some papers, though not mine, as rim rats) to pick up a dummy, find in the computer the sto-

ries the slot had chosen for that page, edit the stories, trim
them to fit, write headlines, crop the photos, and then bring
the page out to the composing room so the printers could
paste it up. And then we would go back to the desk and pick
up another dummy and start again. Page by page, we were
putting together a newspaper.

My summer on the *Herald* copy desk meant coming in
at five in the morning, editing until noon, and then moving over to the library after lunch. My days were long, and
I was sleepy by about three. Sometimes I went back to my
stuffy apartment and took a long nap. I fell very far behind
in my library filing, partly through exhaustion but, frankly,
primarily through lack of interest. I dutifully cut out all of
the stories each day, but I never seemed to get around to
putting them away, and the stash of unfiled clips grew. I hid
it under the front counter, which hung over the edge of my
desk. Sometimes a reporter came in looking for a clip and
I would say, "I'll bring it out to you," in a brisk and efficient
way, and after they were gone, I would haul the pile of clips
out to the middle of my desk and plow through it frantically.

I wasn't worried. I knew that in the fall, once my copy
desk stint ended, I would be able to catch up. Except that I
wasn't; at the end of the summer, they offered me a permanent, full-time job on the *News-Tribune* copy desk, working
4:00 P.M. to 1:00 A.M. I said yes, and immediately decided
that my unfiled clips would become the problem of the new
librarian, whoever that might be. I remember those last two
weeks in the library as blissful, tidying up a bit, cleaning out
my desk, lamenting that I would have to relinquish my giant
pair of deadly scissors, counting down the hours to the end
of tedium and isolation.

The library job drew a lot of applicants; apparently not everyone thought that filing newspaper clippings all day is stultifying work. One afternoon Tom Daly wandered into the library and asked me how the job search was going. "It's going well," I said. "There's a guy downstairs right now in HR, taking the test."

"A guy?" Daly said thoughtfully. "Hmmmm. I wonder what I'd have to do about the pay." And he meandered back out into the newsroom. When I told this story later, over beers at the Pickwick, my friends all had the same reaction: "Sue him! Discrimination!" But I just chuckled. I had something better than a settlement; I had a permanent job on the night copy desk.

The low job on the night desk was handling the state and local stories, so that job fell to me. I found the work interesting but difficult. I had to lay out my own pages, drawing them by hand on the pale green dummy sheets, making accommodations on the fly for stories that came in too long (they never came in too short, for some reason) or that broke late. I remade pages for later runs, killing the wire stories and subbing late local copy. At the same time, I had to monitor the state wires, making sure I found room for whatever was important or newsy. The news came over the wires all night, flowing into segregated computer queues, and I was responsible for three of them: Minn Wire, Wis Wire (where the truly bizarre stories lived), and BC Minn, which meant "both cycles" and filled up at odd times with odd bits of news. Somehow in the crush of handling the new job, my overloaded brain didn't fully register all of this. One night, months into my job, when I didn't have enough news to fill my pages, the slot, John Murrell, said, "Did you check the wires?" "Yeah," I said. "Nothing on Minn or Wis that's any good."

"What's on BC Minn?" he asked, and I looked at him blankly. "BC Minn?" I said. "What's that?" And Murrell and the wire editor, Keith, looked at each other and said, in unison, "Uh oh!" Ah well. If I had missed any big stories, I could always just claim I had run out of space, which was often true. There was always much more interesting news than we ever had room for. Working on the night desk was a constant scramble, and none of my pages ever looked very good. I never quite got the hang of figuring out the measurements, and so my stories seldom squared off like everyone else's. Theirs looked like nicely designed modules planned around an attractive photo, biggest headline at the top of the page, smallest at the bottom. Mine looked like jigsaw puzzles where the pieces had been forced together. Headlines of all fonts showed up all over the page; if it fit, that was miracle enough. Creating order out of the chaos was more than anyone could expect of me.

For first run, we had to be off the floor by either 11:15 P.M. or 11:30 P.M., depending on whether the run was collect or straight. The terms had to do with the webbing of the press; a straight run was for smaller and simpler papers and got the 11:30 start time. A collect run combined sections from a couple of presses and so took longer and started earlier. It was frustrating to get straight runs on the days the paper was small and those extra fifteen minutes weren't crucial. The big papers—Wednesday and Thursday—were always collect runs, and every week we scrambled to get off the floor on time. Sometimes we were urged to beat deadline. "There's snow in the alley," manager Tod Chadwick would

say, by which he meant, "Hurry up." He used the term whenever they wanted us done early for any reason, but "snow in
the alley" originally came from weather concerns—in bad
weather the trucks might have trouble getting out of town
to drop off papers, so you tried to finish early to give them a
head start. Chadwick was a gruff, prickly sort of character,
though kind underneath. He had a fuzz of strawberry blond
curls tighter and more wiry even than mine, and a beautiful
ornamental tin at his desk that I once opened and peered
into, entranced, thinking that perhaps it contained chocolates. An evil smell issued forth: tobacco spit; he liked to
chew while he worked.

Whenever I whistled at my desk—an annoying, tuneless,
mindless habit that sprang from my nervous fear that I was
going to blow deadline—Chadwick snapped, "No whistling
in the newsroom!" It was bad luck, and even though no one
could explain the reason for the superstition, everybody
knew about it; if you forgot and whistled, the reporters and
editors would all look up and frown. (There were several
explanations for the whistling superstition—that whistling
might mask the sound of the urgent bells ringing on the old
wire machine, that a reporter was whistling when the earth-
quake of 1906 hit San Francisco, that whistling just plain
and simple brings bad luck.)

Every night, we went out into the composing room to
watch the printers paste up our pages. The typeset stories
slid out of a machine in long sheets, printed on heavy, high-
gloss paper. Printers cut out the stories with their X-Acto
knives, fed them through rollers that coated the back side
with sticky hot wax, and pressed them onto full-sized
sheets, using our little dummies as guides. We copy editors

stood by, watching, not whistling, ready to show them which lines to cut if a story didn't fit, or to resend type if there was a problem. Sometimes our layouts called for a story to have a box around it, for prominence on the page (or to keep headlines from bumping). In that case, the printer would take down a roll of border tape that hung on the pegboard walls, and tape the outline of the box right to the page. Bits of that tape littered the back shop floor and stuck to the bottoms of our shoes.

When we trimmed stories on the floor, we marked the cuts with sky blue felt-tipped pens—the light blue ink was invisible to the scanner but not to the printers, who then literally trimmed the marked lines out of the story with their knives. This meant that it was easier for them if we trimmed widows, full lines, or entire paragraphs rather than extraneous words here and there, even though that was always my inclination. Trimming a widow was a thing of beauty. The printer would cut off the period and move it over to the new last word of the sentence, balanced on the tip of his knife blade, and stick it right to the page.

Invariably, my pages required a lot of work from the printers. I almost always found that I had measured wrong when I was designing my dummies, and I didn't have enough space for the photo that I had built the page around. That photo that the poor photographer had framed so deliberately would get cropped on the board on deadline, sometimes until there was almost nothing left of it. The printer would slap his pica pole against the photo and slice off the top or bottom with his knife—sometimes again and again. But we had to make room for the words.

"You know the measurement at the top of your story

when you HNJ it?" wire editor Keith Thomsen asked me patiently, when once again my stories didn't fit my layout. "That's a real number. You can trust it." HNJ was an Atex computer command that meant to hyphenate and justify, turning the story from full-screen to long and skinny, the precise width of a newspaper column. Keith clearly had a good relationship with his HNJ numbers. His pages were always elegantly designed, his headlines were snappy, and he seldom had to trim his art. I tried to trust the computer measures, but somehow whenever I was in the composing room, the live type showed only a vague resemblance to the squiggles on my dummy, and the photos seldom fit.

To get photos to fit our layout, we measured them with our pica poles, marking the crops right on the photo in orange grease pencil. Most of us figured out the size using a proportion wheel. This was two disks of plastic marked with measurements—you lined up the picture's actual width on one disk with the width you wanted it to be on the other disk, and the wheel then pointed to what the depth would become and how much the photo would have to shrink. But one copy editor, Virgil Swing, never bothered with the simple cropping wheel. He cropped pictures using a slide rule, the only time I ever saw one put to use outside of a high school classroom.

Pasting up our pages was tricky, fast work for the printers. We copy editors did not help; in fact, we were forbidden to help. If we helped the printers, all work would cease, and you might not get your newspaper the next morning. One touch of live type by an unauthorized hand, and everything would shut down. The printers had a strong union, and if one of us tried to adjust a crooked headline or pick up a

piece of type that had fallen to the floor, the foreman had
the right to ring the bell, stop work, and call all the printers
to chapel. Chapel is what they called their union meeting;
the term dates to the 1500s, when printers took advan-
tage of religious laws that allowed people to stop work and
assemble.

It was my greatest fear that I would inadvertently cause
a work stoppage, and I kept my hands jammed deep in my
pockets whenever I was out on the composing room floor.
The metal bell was large and round and was mounted on
the wall in the back shop, and when the foreman hit it with
a metal stick, you could hear it reverberate throughout
the second floor. That bell governed their day. The printers started work the moment the foreman rang it, and not
before; they stopped immediately when he rang it again.
The bell told them when to go to dinner and when to come
back from dinner. They took their half-hour break every
night at precisely 9:30 P.M., even though deadline was looming. Many, many nights I begged a printer to finish a page
before going on break—we had page deadlines all night
long, and I was often on the verge of being late. But they
never would. The bell rang, they stopped. The bell rang, they
started. The pleas of a hapless young copy editor might be
pitiful, but they weren't powerful. The bell summoned them
back from dinner at 10:00 P.M., which left just a little more
than an hour until deadline. Around 11:00 P.M. or so, it got
very hectic in the back shop, but everyone worked together
and worked hard, and those last few minutes went by fast.
I was always vying to work with Andy Jones or John Fellbaum. You lived and died by which printer pasted up your
pages; there was tremendous skill to what they did. They

had to be able to calculate quickly—measure the story and then divide by the number of columns, to determine how long each leg of type should be so that it would wrap neatly, squared off over two or three or four columns, sometimes around a photograph, which meant the first leg of type was longer than the others. I would watch with admiration as Andy slapped his pica pole down on the type, quickly calculated in his head, and then sliced decisively and accurately—all in a matter of seconds.

Other printers were not so confident; they trembled when they knifed the type, or they got the division wrong and the stories didn't square off. When that happened, they had to knife individual lines of type and move them over, and invariably some of those lines ended up crooked. On nights when we were extremely busy, all of the printers were pressed into working on the news pages. (Some of the older and shakier ones usually spent their evenings pasting up the classified ads, which did not require as much skill.) Every now and then I got an ancient, stooped printer whose biggest nightmare was pasting up the news pages. He had shaky hands, and he got the measurements bollixed up and often had to cut each line individually and move it from column to column; all the while the ash on his trembling cigarette was growing longer and longer, and I feared it would fall onto my page and get stuck in the wax.

By then, Andy had finished his pages, and he stood by watching with amusement. I kept shooting desperate looks his way, and finally he came over. "I'll take it from here," he said, and Langley gratefully abandoned my page and went back to pasting up the classifieds. Even Andy couldn't get all of those lines of type straight, and it was too late in the evening for me to send the story through again, but at least we got off the floor.

The big unknown every night was class slop. The classified ad department continued selling ads until 7:00 P.M., and it was always pretty late before we knew how many pages those ads would eat up. They would give us a rough estimate early in the evening, and Keith would get a few interesting but not crucial wire stories ready to plop on the pages if needed. And if I ran out of room in the local section, I could use class slop for my makeover. We generally planned for a two-column hole. The printers pasted up the classified section starting with the last page and working backwards, so the first page—the page the classified ads slopped over onto—was a great unknown until right around deadline. Every now and then the ads fell way short, and nothing slopped over. Then Keith would head down the hall toward the copy desk at a dead run. "Open page on class slop!" he would holler, and Murrell would look up from where he was putting the final touches on Page One and say mildly, "House ad?"

And sometimes that was the way we'd go—just slap in a full-page promo touting the wonders of the *News-Tribune,* if it was late and we were crunched and the wires were quiet. But more often Keith would sit down at his tube and start scrolling through the queues, and if we were done with our pages, those of us on the rim would help, and the next morning, perhaps to their surprise, readers would get a full page of late-breaking wire stories, beautifully designed, with two pieces of art, deep in the second section, way back by the classified ads. It was a point of pride to fill that page, even at the last minute, even on the fly. A news hole was precious, and you didn't ever want to waste it.

After deadline, the copy editors took a break, leaned back in their chairs, and chatted. Sometimes Walt Dodge, the venerable rxedit, told stories about World War II. (The job known as "rxedit" was to give a final read to every single story that went into the paper. Walt caught a lot of errors.) "When I was in the service," he would begin, and everyone would pull their chairs closer to listen. Everyone except me; I almost always had makeovers. We published three editions—the Iron Range was printed the earliest; then the Superior, Wisconsin, edition, which circulated as far east as the Upper Peninsula of Michigan; and latest of all was the city run. We tended not to remake the pages with national and international news, but the local news pages often were remade, with late-meeting stories from the city council or school board, or late-breaking crime news. I would rework my pages as fast as I could, listening with one ear to the relaxed banter of the other night editors, eager to join in the conversation. Walt's stories were the best; he had been a wheelsman on a destroyer in the South Pacific, in a convoy that was sent to Malta early in the war. They had to run through a gauntlet of German and Italian submarines, and Walt claimed to have survived three ship sinkings in twenty-four hours. His ship was also down among the atolls when the U.S. government conducted a nuclear weapons test, and when detonation time came close, the ships in the area were given the order to retreat. But Walt's commander gave the opposite order: "Full steam ahead!" And they raced toward the imminent explosion, to get a better view. Perhaps not surprisingly, Walt had a lot of health problems.

The night copy editors were a brilliant bunch, intelligent and funny and sarcastic, with sharp-edged observations and great black humor. They talked about everything, with the intimacy that came from the quiet late-night newsroom and the shared stress of intense work and odd hours; not only did we work nights, but we usually worked weekends and holidays as well. After first run, we played word games and held quizzes; one night the topic was music, and I stumped them all with this question: "Who was the biscuit who went west?" (Answer: Rudy Darling, of the original Powdermilk Biscuit Band.) The other copy editors were not yet *Prairie Home Companion* fans, and they stared at me as though I had lost my mind. "Music," said Pam Miller. "The topic is music. Not food."

One night the topic turned to sex: What were the circumstances of our first time? Everyone told, and if I could remember the stories, I would tell them here, but, sadly, I don't, not any of them, though I do remember that all of them were funny. One copy editor continued to click away at his keyboard—clearing wires, I assumed, or handling some late-breaking story. But Murrell was suspicious. "Say, uh, Peter, what you working on over there, Buddy?" he asked. Peter, a redheaded recent graduate of Brown University, didn't even turn around. "I'm taking notes," he said, "for my novel." (Yes, yes, we let him live. But we also made him delete the file.)

Working on local copy meant editing long boring stories about the city council, and eye-glazing stories about issues that were important but didn't necessarily make good reading: The International Joint Commission and its governance of Lake Superior water (McMillion's pet topic; he had been ahead of the curve); Our Disappearing Wetlands; the Iron Range Resources and Rehabilitation Board (known as the Eye-Triple-R-B) and its efforts to bring some

kind of industry to northern Minnesota, any industry, anything at all, to replace the vanishing taconite plants. One
Saturday evening I had to copyedit an unfathomable story
about peatlands up north; I couldn't follow what it was
about, exactly, but it had already been through the city desk,
and I figured the problem was me: I must be stupid. The
reporter walked by. "My story OK?" she asked. "Yep," I said,
with a false heartiness that I hoped masked my befuddle-
ment. "Looks good."

"Great," she said, walking away, "because I have absolutely no idea what it was about."

This stopped me in mid-edit. A little epiphany. Hmm.
*If I don't understand it, perhaps the readers won't under-
stand it either.* It occurred to me that maybe I wasn't stupid; maybe all those stories that made my eyes droop truly
were boring, and maybe all those stories that went over my
head really were poorly written and badly organized. I had
always assumed the flaw was in me, that somehow I just
wasn't concentrating, but maybe the flaw was in the stories themselves. I had always loved writing, but I had never
considered newspapers to be *written*, exactly, so much as
just pounded out by formula. But perhaps the writing was
important after all.

The copy desk job that I coveted was Keith's job, sorting
wires; I loved reading the different stories that flowed into
our computers all night long from all over the world. The
early versions from the Associated Press were terse and
just the facts. The later the night went, the richer and better
told the stories became. The Duluth paper was part of the
Knight-Ridder chain, known then as the Cadillac of newspaper chains, and the stories on the Knight-Ridder wire

were well worth waiting for, but they were also the hardest to get into the paper. They came in late, and they were quite long and so beautifully crafted that they were hard to cut— complicated, dramatic tales from the *Philadelphia Inquirer* and the *Detroit Free Press* and the *Miami Herald.* These were not stories you could just knife from the bottom if they were too long, in the tradition of the inverted pyramid. These were full stories, with beginnings, middles, endings. *If I ever become a reporter, those are the kinds of stories I'm going to do,* I thought. But of course, that was silly; I was never going to become a reporter. I was quite content where I was. With copyediting, I had found my calling. I had the excitement and adrenaline of deadlines and breaking news, I knew everything that was going on, and at night there were no managers around to bug us. Pam, Murrell, Keith, and I were all only in our twenties or early thirties, but after about seven, we called all the shots.

Keith Thomsen was the wire editor, also known as the "inside slot." He was a witty and sarcastic counterpoint to our Page One slot, John Murrell, who was also witty and sarcastic. (By now the previous witty and sarcastic Page One slot, Bill Sniffen, had moved on to the *Philadelphia Inquirer,* taking our nightside clerk with him as his wife.) Murrell was tall and thin with glasses and a small mustache; he looked just like James Thurber but was, possibly, even wryer. He knew that I had my eye on Keith's job, so when Keith was on vacation, Murrell trained me in as backup. Sorting wires was great fun and great responsibility. There was never enough room for all the news we wanted to run, and so you had to be judicious. Every inch of space was precious. Sometimes stories that we thought deeply important ended up as briefs or didn't make the paper at all. But I loved the nights I sorted wires because I got to read everything that came in, whether it made print or not. I have never been so well-informed as I was in those years.

The inside slot read each story and assigned it a priority: Y for yes (meaning it must get in); M for maybe (I always had about a thousand maybes; I couldn't help it; everything was interesting); B for brief it; and N for no. We also had O for oddball, but I never figured out how to find room for the O's when there were still so many Y's, B's, and M's to fit in. As I sorted, Murrell looked over my shoulder and tweaked my priorities. One night a wire story moved late with an URGENT label and a lede that said that British warships were steaming toward the Falkland Islands. Warships! This sounded important, even though I had no idea where the Falkland Islands might be. I marked it with a Y. Murrell chuckled. He took a drag on his cigarette and said, "You might want to just brief that one." I blushed and changed the priority. The next morning the Falkland War was all over the news. Ah well, at least we had that brief. When I got in to work, Murrell apologized. "You called that one right," he said. But really, I hadn't. It had just been a guess.

It was Murrell's calm guidance that taught me news judgment—his and Linda Ellerbee's. Every night I went home and turned on *NBC News Overnight* to compare what she had chosen for her broadcast with what I had chosen for the morning paper. Sometimes my stomach sank as Ellerbee trumpeted a story that I had rejected as an M (the M's almost never cracked the paper) or had blown off as a B. Sometimes she and I were completely in sync, and I would curl up on the couch chuckling as she went through her story list, watching as it matched mine, story for story for story. I would shout at the TV: "I got that one! I got that one!"

Working on the copy desk also taught me to recognize the fundamentals of a news story—the lede (the opening), the nut graf (a summary of the story's main points), the background and context and support, the powerful quotes, the various points of view, the kicker at the end. I didn't yet have terms for any of those things, but I got so that I could tell at a quick read when a story lacked something it needed. Copyediting was more than just fixing typos and trimming stories in a panic on deadline in the back shop. The heart of the job was reading the stories and making sure they had what they needed for publication. And the fact that a story came from a wire service didn't mean it was beyond question; many nights I heard Murrell on the phone to an editor at the Minneapolis or New York Associated Press desks, asking questions about sourcing or context.

The paper came out every day, and so in addition to working nights I worked weekends and most holidays, and for long spans of time I had split days off—Tuesdays and Thursdays. I didn't care a bit. I loved going to work at four; I would get up at ten and feel like I had an entire day to squander before walking in the front door of the *News-Tribune*. Pam Miller and I would go cross-country skiing along the trails at Hartley Field (sometimes getting lost) or hiking out at Jay Cooke State Park, or I would stop by the big gray house on Fourth Street to visit my parents, or I would climb onto my old orange bike and pedal up the Shore. Copyediting was a job where you started fresh every day, worked like a dog for nine or ten hours, and then went home and left it all behind. You couldn't carry over your work from day to day, because everything had to be finished before you left. It made for a stressful day, but it meant you could generally leave work behind when you walked out the door at midnight. Still, there were tensions. Murrell told me that one night he sat bolt upright in bed at four in the morning, suddenly hit by the cold fear that he had misspelled a word in the main headline on Page One. He couldn't get back to sleep unless he knew for sure. So he sat up until five, when the papers were delivered to the convenience stores, and then he called the 7-Eleven. "Do me a favor," he told the clerk. "Can you look at the headline on the front page and tell me how 'judgment' is spelled?"

The clerk read it to him: J-U-D-G-E-M-E-N-T.

There was nothing else for Murrell to do but go back to bed.

Perhaps the worst mistake I observed came when one of the other rimmers was filling in as slot. We were running a moving Knight-Ridder tale out of the Southwest about illegal immigrants, and the word she used in the headline, stripped across the top of Page One was this: "Wetbacks." She was enormously upset and embarrassed the next day when she got to work and found out what the word meant—and how angry people were. "I had no idea it was a slur!" she kept saying. "I thought it was just a shorter way to say migrant worker!"

I would have been perfectly happy to stay on the copy desk forever. But one thing about newsrooms: they don't stay static for long. Top management had changed again; Daly and Knaus had moved on—Daly to California, and Knaus to the *Boulder Daily Camera*—Jack Tyllia and Fritz Nothacker were no longer the city editors; and we had a new executive editor, a slow-talking, pipe-smoking, bearded guy named Larry Fortner who had come here from Indiana by way of Florida and Kentucky. Between Fortner and Daly, we had had a brief tenure of a guy some of us nicknamed "the Barracuda"—not only did he have very big white teeth under a porn-star mustache, but even to my innocent eyes it was clear that he was a climber. You could tell by the cut of his suit and by the sweeping and dramatic changes he instituted that Duluth was a springboard to bigger and better places. He swept in, redesigned the paper, ordered up themed sections, and reallocated the staff to fill them. He put Tyllia in charge of making the whole thing work, despite Tyllia's protestations that we didn't have the news hole or the staff to sustain it all. And then he was gone, swept on out to a bigger paper somewhere else, and Tyllia and the new guy, Fortner, were left to slowly dismantle the Barracuda's changes.

This was the first time I had witnessed this—someone instituting changes that they must have known were impossible, using those changes as evidence of their great skill, and then parlaying them into a fabulous job, leaving others behind to fix the mess. But it was not the last time I saw it. This turned out to be a common occurrence in my years in journalism, and the only thing astounding about it was the fact that it almost always worked. Journalists deal in facts and truth; we can be prosaic to a fault. And consequently not a lot of us are blessed with creativity and vision—we're too busy toiling. Perhaps when someone comes along who appears to be a big thinker, someone with ideas, it's so impressive that we're blinded. Who knows? But I have seen this over and over, and the only surprise is that it continues to work.

Fortner showed up in 1980, not a dreamer, but a news guy who had started out in sports, where you have to be fast and lively and pay attention to deadline. Up until now, newspapers had been swimming in money, earning record profits, but things were starting to change. All over the country, afternoon papers were shutting down as people switched from reading an evening paper to watching the evening news on TV. Down in the Twin Cities, the afternoon *Star* and the morning *Tribune* had merged, folding together two highly competitive newsrooms. Across the river, the afternoon *St. Paul Dispatch* shut down, merging with the morning *Pioneer Press*.

Rumors about our own future had been flying for weeks, and it was a difficult but not entirely unexpected day when Fortner called the staff together to announce the merger of the *Herald* and the *News-Tribune*. The afternoon *Herald* would cease publication, he said, but we would retain its features in a bigger, better morning paper. The *News-Tribune & Herald* (as the paper was now to be called) would carry both sets of comics, Dear Abby and Ann Landers, and both crossword puzzles. And so it did—for a year, and then the order for more cuts came down from above. Merging the *News-Tribune* and *Herald* was not terribly traumatic from where I sat; while the company lost about two dozen jobs overall, none were from the newsroom. Most of the reporters worked for both papers anyway, writing one version of their story quickly for the *Herald* and then reworking it late into the evening for the next morning's *News-Tribune*. One reporter viewed the merger as a good thing: "I won't have to write the same story twice every day," he said, which remained true until the Internet came along. But it was the first inkling that papers weren't going to grow indefinitely; it was the first experience I had with scaling back.

By now Murrell was dating a reporter—a vague, charmingly inarticulate, lovely young woman who could not make deadline. Diane panicked prettily, couldn't get her stories written, and was in danger of losing her job. Fortner had already told her to forget about first run; just write for second run. But she couldn't make second run either. It wasn't the time of the deadline that paralyzed her; it was the presence of any deadline at all.

So Murrell and Fortner talked. And when he came out of Fortner's office, Murrell called a quick meeting of the copy desk to announce a new standard: all copy editors need to have reporting experience. Heads slowly swiveled until everyone was looking at me. Pam Miller, Keith Thomsen, Walt Dodge, Dave Butters—each of them had done reporting at one time or another. Even Dick Gerzic had written a bowling column for our sports pages. All of them had been reporters in one way or another, except me.

Murrell nodded in my direction. Diane would take my spot on the desk. I would move to days and to writing. I would cover the Iron Range. I felt myself grow pale. I was terribly shy, I had only recently learned to drive, I still hadn't finished college, I had never been to the Iron Range, I had no desire to go out into the world and talk to strangers. *This was not part of the deal!*

"You start next week," he said. "You'll report to John Krebs."

And so I was dragged, silently screaming, into the world of reporting.

•

An Accidental Reporter

WHEN IT COMES RIGHT DOWN TO IT, I DID EVERY-thing wrong. You're supposed to actively choose journalism as your career. Then you go to J school (as journalism majors call it), work on the college newspaper, get a couple of internships under your belt, and graduate. (Graduating is kind of key.) After that, you go work at a weekly or a small daily, hop to a slightly larger paper, maybe go to grad school. Eventually, you end up at the big time.

This is not how I did it, and this is not how the old guys I worked with had done it. They had fallen into journalism after careers in public relations or teaching or tending bar or, one of them, after serving a term or two as mayor of Duluth. Journalism was seen, in those years, as a craft—something any smart and curious person could learn on the job. But by the mid-1980s, when Larry Fortner callously tossed me over to the reporting side, journalism had become a profession, with a very distinct and proper career path. By then we had a new batch of young, college-educated reporters and editors: Chris Ison had worked for the *Minnesota Daily* at the University of Minnesota before Fortner hired him to cover the city of Superior. Doug Smith had worked up in Ely, at the weekly *Echo*, before coming to Duluth to cover the environment. Pam Miller earned her master's degree at the University of Minnesota Duluth while working on the night copy desk.

Not me. I never did any of those things. I never intended to be a journalist, never meant to be a reporter, never moved around the country, never quite finished college. Everything I did, I did by accident and happenstance. My motto was: When a door opens, walk through it. But I didn't spend a lot of time worrying about picking the door. I toiled away at whatever job came my way—clerk, librarian, copy editor—having a pretty good time, doing some interesting stuff, never exactly getting around to choosing a career. I had spent a year at the College of St. Scholastica before starting at the paper. Then, when I worked days as a clerk, I took night classes at UMD (which many of my East End high school friends had scorned as "grade thirteen"), and when I worked nights on the desk, I took day classes. My majors were English and history, but I also took a bunch of other random classes just because they sounded fun. I ignored most of the general ed requirements. This was exactly contrary to the advice I had gotten from my high school guidance counselor. He told me that he had spent several extra and unnecessary years in college because he took classes that sounded interesting but didn't count toward a degree. He said, "Don't make the mistake I did." And I secretly thought, "That sounds like a great way to go to college!" And that is what I did.

I took a full year of Latin. I took a reading French class where we never learned to pronounce anything, but by the end of spring semester I was laboriously plowing through *Alice au Pays des Merveilles* in my parents' backyard, with the help of a thick French-English dictionary, figuring it was easier to translate a book I had already read in English. I took every writing class I could get my hands on, and I took a ton of history classes. I took art appreciation and learned about fur-lined teacups and Dadaism, and I took a summer class called The Changing Roles of Women, in which I learned to stand up for myself and not be kept down by the Man (or, in this case, Men). To make her point, the professor treated the two male students in the class the way that women had traditionally been treated; that is, she interrupted them, belittled their answers, and dismissed what they had to say. It was pretty easy to figure out what she was doing, but instead of making her point, she ended up infuriating most of the women in the class, who seemed to have a strong sense of fairness—or perhaps a strong need to protect men.

All of this was interesting. None of it was immediately useful or practical, and very little of it counted toward a degree. I didn't care; I had lots of time, didn't I? I was only in my mid—well, by now, late twenties. I had lots of time to pick a career and finish school. So instead, I read a lot, and took up long-distance running, and went cross-country skiing in the winter and backpacking in the autumn, and after a while I got a dog, and it was all quite fun and interesting, and I was curious to see where life would take me next.

And what did life do? It opened a door and shoved me through, and I came out the other side a reporter.

After I stopped panicking, the first thing I did was buy myself one of those pinstriped charcoal gray suits and a silky blouse that tied in a big soft bow at the throat. Hey, it was the eighties, and I knew from watching *L.A. Law* that

that was what career women wore, even though not a single woman in the newsroom dressed like that. And neither did I, after my first or second week. It just wasn't practical, since you often didn't know where you would be sent or what kind of story you might have to report. It's hard to ride a snow-mobile out to the middle of a frozen lake to view plane crash wreckage, for instance, in a narrow pinstripe skirt and a blouse with a bow.

I got my own desk, my own red phone, a reporter's note-book, and access to the staff cars. The notebook was long and skinny—good to jam into a back pocket, I assume, but a bit long for most purses—and it said, in blue letters on the white cardboard front, PROFESSIONAL REPORTER'S NOTEBOOK. I was deeply impressed with myself and my new accoutrements and proudly showed the notebook to a friend, who burst out laughing and said, "It looks like something you'd buy to go with a Halloween costume!"

I had only just learned to drive, taught by my mother, who took me on the winding lanes of Park Hill Cemetery up in Woodland where I couldn't kill anyone, because they were already dead. I had acquired a sporty-looking second-hand Chevy Monza, yellow, with a dashing orange pinstripe. It was sporty in looks alone, though, and had sluggish pickup that made me forever wary of merging on freeways ("C'mon c'mon c'mon c'mON!") and rear-wheel drive that was almost useless in the winter; I used to get stuck regu-larly in two inches of snow. Still, I could drive, and in the nick of time, since I was now not just a reporter but a roving reporter who covered the Iron Range—hundreds of miles of small towns, deep forests, taconite mines, and a slowly shrinking economy. Just like Jacqui Banaszynski! Only much shorter. And a lot less confident.

By now, Jacqui had moved on to the *Portland Oregonian*. Most of those other young women had moved on as well—Suzanne Perry was reporting in Belgium, Sue Willoughby had gone to work for a state senator, and Ruth Hammond was down in the Twin Cities, writing her long, beautiful pieces for the Minneapolis paper. A lot of the old men had retired—Les Ormandy, the business writer who gave me his old books, had left without saying a word. On the day of his retirement, he just lifted his baggy raincoat off the coatrack at the end of the day as he always did, and walked out the door.

The newsroom was full of new hires, bright and aggressive young reporters who took the job seriously. We had an entertainment writer named Bob Ashenmacher who kept his cigarettes rolled up in the sleeve of his white T-shirt and smoked cigars when he was writing late reviews; he was all of twenty-five years old and never seemed to notice our snickers when he earnestly told his editor that he was "hard on deadline."

Along the way I had somehow briefly acquired a husband; he was about as cute and inappropriate as my Chevy Monza, though frankly the Monza served me better and lasted longer. He was a sweet, boyish college student who looked remarkably like the actor Scott Baio and whose mother was dying, a sad fact that lent him an irresistibly tragic and vulnerable air. He had the unlikely and unwieldy last name of Schleppenbach, which I promptly made even more unlikely and unwieldy by sticking to my teenage conviction that marriage is a partnership and a woman should honor that partnership by hyphenating her name. I regretted it almost immediately, when I saw that it forced my byline onto two lines. Murrell pointed out that mine was not the only two-line byline out there—the Associated Press employed a writer with the lyrical name Scheherezade Faramarzi—and then he promptly started calling me Hertzbach.

On the regional desk, I worked for John Krebs. He was slow moving and gray haired, with eyes that looked at the world, or at least at me, with benevolent amusement. He had been a reporter, he had been a copy editor, he had been a city editor, and now he was the regional editor, choosing the stories that we would write from all over our vast coverage area—not just the Iron Range and the North Shore but northwestern Wisconsin and the Upper Peninsula of Michigan too. He had to be judicious. Because of the distances, it was hard to cover news as it happened; unless it was something we could get by phone, we generally used Associated Press stories for the first day and then went on the road and did our own second-day story or weekender.

He started me off easy. My first assignment was to write a back-to-school feature story about an elderly woman who made a living by renting rooms to college students. She had been doing this for so many years that everyone on campus knew her, and she had been invited to countless weddings and christenings. She preferred male renters to female—less trouble, apparently, and they also shoveled the walk. OK, not the best story you ever read in your paper, but I was a brand-new reporter, and we had space to fill. So, with trembling fingers, I punched in her number on the phone.

"Hellooo?" came her quavery voice, and I answered her in a voice just as quavery. I took a deep breath, started over, and blurted, "This is Laurie Hertzel-Schleppenbach from the *News-Tribune & Herald*." There was a pause. Then the woman said, "Honey, I can't understand a word you just said." And I believe it is to my credit that I didn't just slam down the phone and go tell Krebs, sorry, no story; the woman is dead.

The staff cars lived in the garage under our building and were allegedly maintained by a crabby garageman named Frank. We called him Frahnk. He had names for some of us too; he called Bob Ashenmacher "Batman," which was apt; Bob was always running late and used to rush into the garage in great haste, his raincoat flapping like a cape, hop into the reportermobile, and peel out into the alley like a—well, like a bat out of hell. It was clear that Frahnk had no respect for him, or for any of us. We didn't have a lot of respect for Frahnk, either; the staff cars were chronically low on gas, usually full of cigarette butts and food wrappers, and often had wires and odd bits of metal poking out of the seats, which ripped the stockings of any woman foolish enough to wear stockings to work. (One reporter tried to expense a new pair after her legs were gouged by a car seat, but her claim was denied.) Even though Frahnk was there ostensibly to maintain the cars, no maintenance was ever done on them by him or his predecessor, as far as we could tell. One January, Jacqui drove all the way to Canada in a car with no heat.

Parking in that garage was an endless source of terror to me. I was still new at this driving business—until just a year or two before, I had ridden my bike everywhere, even to the Laundromat, with my dirty clothes stuffed into two red pannier bags—and I was not at all confident maneuvering in and out of tiny spaces in an underground cavern that had support beams every ten feet, no room to turn around, and Frahnk watching balefully from his chair by the door.

You could tell from his expression that he was just waiting for you to hit something. Sometimes he would watch with something like contempt as I backed up and pulled out and backed up again, and he would finally say, "I'll park it for you," and I would leap out in relief, the engine still running, grab my notebook, and flee to the newsroom.

The staff cars said DULUTH NEWS-TRIBUNE & HERALD, stenciled in big white letters on the doors in the same font as our flag. This charmed me for about a week—*Look at me driving around! I work for the press!*—until it became apparent that being incognito was a much more efficient way to do business. We had one unmarked car, and it was much in demand. All of the cars were American-made, to ensure no trouble when we went up to the Iron Range, where jobs were being lost by the hundreds to foreign steel. The cars were equipped with two-way radios, so you could communicate with the newsroom while on the road. It was very Star Trek—the radio was a bulky beige box that was mounted on the console next to the automatic shift; you had to depress a key on the walkie-talkie to speak, and then release it to hear the response. One morning someone accidentally depressed the key with her leg when she was adjusting the car seat. The transmit key remained depressed for her hour-long drive to Biwabik, and so her voice was beamed into the newsroom, singing, singing, singing along with the radio as she zipped up Highway 53. It was a cheerful sound, and it lifted our spirits for the whole afternoon.

Krebs usually spent his afternoons perusing the weekly papers from the Iron Range and northern Wisconsin. Every so often, he would clip out a story and lumber over to my desk and tell me to go report and write my own version.

When I went on the road, I always had at least two assignments, to make the best use of time and gasoline, usually one newsy story and one feature. Good stories, stupid stories, stories about people who made crafts in their senior citizen apartments, stories about women who raised llamas, stories about kids with sad untreatable diseases, or Native American women who braided rugs to sell, or artists who lived in the middle of nowhere, stories about the Last Cobbler of Barnum, or the last appliance repair shop, or the last mom-and-pop resort, or the last we'll-pump-it-for-you gas station—for a stretch of about three years I specialized in what I called End of an Era stories. Eras were ending left and right, and I wrote about them all. I also got the newsy stories—taconite plants shutting down, unemployment rising, people moving away, strikes at the mines, school districts consolidating. And every now and then, a plane crash, a tornado, a flood, a fire, a murder.

My first out-of-the-office reporting assignment was a story about how new security cameras had been installed in the hallways of Proctor High School. I was teamed up with a photographer named John Rott who was the epitome of calm, and I would not have made it through that assignment without him. He was one of the most laid-back people I've ever worked with. I don't know if he picked up on my nervousness—maybe he thought I always trembled and my voice always rose to little more than a squeak. In any case, he didn't say anything about it. He just drove us to Proctor, went into the interview with me, lounged quietly in his chair, and whenever I was struck dumb by nervousness, which was frequently, he filled in the gap by asking some basic question that should have occurred to me.

I asked the principal everything I could think of, and
then Rott and I went out into the hall and talked to students.
No one seemed very concerned about the cameras; no one
seemed to view them as any kind of civil liberties infringe-
ment. There wasn't very much crime or trouble in the halls
of Proctor High School anyway. Rott took some pictures,
and then we drove back to the office. I spent the afternoon
poring over my notes, calling the principal back to ask
things I should have asked earlier, and quietly panicking at
my desk. Finally I got up and walked over to Krebs. "I can't
think of anything else to ask anybody," I said.

He looked up at me, his round face amused. "Then I'd
say it's time for you to write your story," he said.

Ah. Oh yeah. *Write.* I slunk back to my desk and booted
up my computer. *Write.*

While I loved the character of the newsroom, I loved the
characters who populated it even more. One aging copy
editor spent his dinner breaks at the bar of the Chinese Lantern, the restaurant down the block. He would come back
fairly incapable of working copy, but nobody ever said anything, because he wasn't that much more competent when
he was sober. He got picked up for drunk driving once,
and he showed up at work the day of his court appearance
dressed in his nicest navy blue sport coat. It had an impressive gold crest embroidered on the breast pocket, and it
wasn't until we looked closer that we realized that it was the
Jack Daniel's logo. We never asked, but we often wondered
how that went over with the judge.

There was that bright young man from Brown University who worked on the night desk. He had no interest at

all in copyediting; he wanted to be a writer. He would race through his pages every night and then go hang out with the reporters, bugging them and asking if he could tag along on assignment. He had a crush on the lovely Diane, and one night after first run he walked over to her desk and left a note on her keyboard. Then he put on his coat and went home. Murrell and I had been sitting at the copy desk, chatting and surreptitiously keeping an eye on him. "Hmmm," Murrell said. He walked over to Diane's desk, picked up the note, and read it. "Interesting," he said. "Too bad she'll never see it." And he crumpled it up and threw it in the trash. Wow! What a bold move! Just like in the movies!

There was a youthful white-haired business writer who used to hang out in the library and tell me that chocolate chip cookies were better than sex. Did his wife know he felt that way, I wondered, and did she bake cookies for him often?

A new managing editor came in and told Richard L. "I Cover the Waterfront" Pomeroy that it was a conflict of interest for him to work on the docks each November, since he covered the docks the eleven other months of the year. Pomeroy was incensed. He quit soon after, crossed the river, and began working for the *Superior Evening Telegram*, which did not have similar concerns.

And the parties . . . oh, the parties. We worked hard together all day, and then got together to drink and talk all night. You would think we would be sick of each other, but no. We dated each other, fought with each other, broke up with each other, drank some more. Our favorite haunts were the Pioneer Bar, kitty-corner from the newspaper, where the cops hung out; the Anchor Bar in Superior ($2 pitchers on Monday nights, also known as Philosophy Night); and the Pickwick, which had German beer on tap, colored-glass windows, and taxidermy displays hanging from the ceiling and walls.

More than once, feature writer Katy Read and I stopped at the Pickwick for dinner and ran into one or two or ten other newsroom folks there, usually sitting at the big round wooden table over on the bar side. Sometimes we would see Gordy Behrens, our thin and elderly bon vivant food writer who had once lived in France; he wore three-piece suits and cavalierly took taxicabs to all his assignments. He waved to us from the bar but refused to join us, and once when Katy and I got ready to leave, we found that he had paid for our dinner.

Katy and I lived just a couple of blocks apart in the reporters' ghetto; I lived in a brick apartment building across the avenue from the Patty Cake Shop and often awoke to the fragrance of Sacher torte wafting in my window. Katy lived on the ground floor of a big yellow house on First Street, just three blocks away. On Fridays, when the weather was nice, we sometimes beer-walked home; that is, we stopped at the Pioneer and the Pickwick and Sir Ben's along the way. By the time we got home, we were usually quite happy and sometimes rather sleepy. Sometimes Bob Allen, the low-key, lanky reporter who covered St. Louis County government, walked with us. On the night of my twenty-ninth birthday, the three of us stopped at Sir Ben's, and Katy dug around in her backpack and pulled out a gift. I began to cry. This was not exactly the reaction they were expecting, despite the fact that we had beer-walked to three different bars, which sometimes had the effect of making

me emotional. I was getting divorced, I said. My marriage
to Scott Baio had lasted barely four years, two of which he
had spent going to school at the U in the Twin Cities and,
um, acquiring a girlfriend. (Should I be shattered or flat-
tered by the fact that she had curly hair just like mine?) It's
true that I had spent those four years working nights, working days, working weekends, working holidays, driving all
over the Iron Range, sometimes on overnight assignments,
and working late at the drop of a hat, sometimes night after
night after night. Oh yeah and beer-walking home with
Katy. But all journalists live like this, and they don't all get
divorced. Do they? I didn't think I would miss him all that
much, but I felt like a failure: I was almost thirty, and I was
about to be single again.

Bob looked uncomfortable at these revelations (he had a
wife and daughter waiting for him at home), but Katy knew
just what to say. "Thank God," she said. "You can finally
have a normal byline."

·

Up the Shore

MURRELL WAS LEAVING.

Pam Miller had already left, screeching her blue car to the curb one Saturday afternoon when she saw me walking along First Street, and hollering happily out the window, "I got a job in Anchorage! I'm moving to Alaska!" After she peeled back out into traffic, I started to cry. She and I had backpacked on Isle Royale together, gotten lost cross-country skiing on the web of trails in Hartley Field, taken endless hikes up the North Shore and in Jay Cooke State Park. She had been my friendly guide as I learned the ways of the copy desk, defended my messy pages to the printers, taught me to recycle my pop cans, brought in cookie bars for my birthday. She had me over to her house and made me tofu stroganoff. ("It tastes just like meat!") (It tasted nothing like meat.) We went out to dinner every Monday night, getting big virtuous salads and then stopping at Fanny Farmer to bring back chocolates for the copy desk. Once we left a truffle for city editor Doug Smith, who was in a meeting, and by the time he got back to his desk, it had melted all over his keyboard. We heard his aggrieved shouts; we kept our heads down and never confessed. Pam had recently gotten married to another grad student in a sunny ceremony in the flower gardens of Enger Tower, and I had known that her departure was just a matter of time. I had known that she was looking. But I was crushed when she left.

And now Murrell. He had landed a job on the copy desk of the *San Jose Mercury News* in California. I didn't understand this; why did everyone want to move on? What was wrong with Duluth that made everybody leave? It's true that when people left, there was always a new batch of energetic young reporters ready to replace them. But I felt like I had to keep making new best friends as old ones left, and I didn't understand why people weren't content to stay. The new hires mostly came from the Twin Cities; they were forever driving back to Minneapolis for their weekends, which I found annoying. I saw it as a lack of commitment to Duluth and an insult to the wonders of where we worked and lived—the funky bars, the omnipresent lake, the wild, wooded parks scattered all over town, the small but intense hippie population you could always find measuring out legumes from burlap sacks at the Fourth Street co-op, or drinking imported beer at Sir Ben's, or contra dancing at the YWCA (usually sixteen or seventeen enthusiastic women in clogs and Peruvian sweaters, and two or three skinny, bearded men).

Who needed the Cities? We had at least three restaurants, maybe more (Sir Ben's, the Pickwick, and Hacienda del Sol); our own comedy troupe ("Colder by the Lake"); an earnest group of young poets who published anthologies (*Poets Who Haven't Moved to Minneapolis* and its sequel, *Poets Who Haven't Moved to St. Paul*); and while we didn't have much original music (Bob Dylan had fled early; the musicians of Low had barely yet been born), sometimes

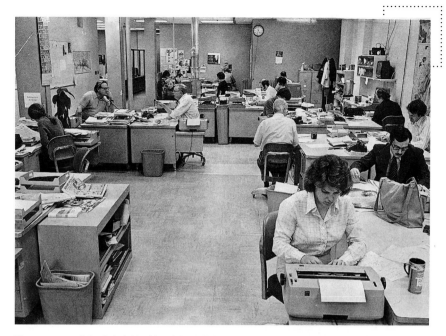

The newsroom of the *Duluth Herald* and the *Duluth News-Tribune* was a crammed and cluttered place in March 1978. *Left to right:* Laurie Hertzel (with braid); Richard L. "I Cover the Waterfront" Pomeroy (on phone); former Duluth mayor George D. Johnson (across from Pomeroy); religion reporter Bob Hull (in white shirt, back to camera); reporter Sue Willoughby (typing, drinking Tab); legislative reporter Paul S. Brissett (in glasses and tie); Superior reporter Irv Mossberger (behind Brissett); reporter and former city editor Janet Burns (behind Mossberger). The city desk is in the background, with *Herald* city editor Fritz Nothacker in the center of the picture (head turned away from the camera) and *News-Tribune* city editor Jack Tyllia to the right (balding head, white shirt). Way, way, way in the back are Jacqui Banaszynski and Keith Thomsen.

Newsroom clerk Laurie Hertzel became the newsroom librarian in 1978. It would be another couple of years before she unfurled her hair.

The copy desk of the *Duluth News-Tribune*, circa 1982: John Murrell *(front)*, Pamela Miller, Keith Thomsen, Sylvia Wier, Walt Dodge, Dick Gerzic, Laurie Hertzel *(back)*. This photograph was taken for a house ad, promoting the copy desk as "The women and men behind the headlines."

On the Iron Range in 1984, reporting a story about a woman who raised llamas. During the early 1980s, I covered northern Minnesota, northwestern Wisconsin, and Upper Michigan, and a photographer and I usually went on the road once or twice a week. Each road trip had to yield at least two stories. *Photograph by Joey McLeister.*

Photographer John Rott and I were assigned to follow a rural mail carrier during a busy Christmas delivery season. Halfway through our day my ears started to freeze, and Rott kindly lent me his hat. *Photograph by John Rott.*

Talking with students at Morgan Park school in Duluth for a feature story, 1985. Twenty-five years ago, interviewing students was simple: a reporter could just show up and freely talk to kids on the school grounds or even in the hallways. Rules became stricter as time went on, and now reporters need advance permission from the principal as well as from parents. *Photograph by Bob King.*

In 1986 consumer goods were so scarce in Leningrad that when Russian people saw a line, they joined it—often before they knew what the line was for. This queue, near the Museum of the History of Religion and Atheism (the former Kazan Cathedral) was for ice cream. *Photograph by Joey McLeister.*

Mayme Sevander in her apartment in Petrozavodsk in 1986, with her grandson, Andy. She was telling us about an Ice Capades performance she had attended fifteen years before in the United States. Of all the American Finns we met in Petrozavodsk, Sevander was the only one who had been allowed to visit America. *Photograph by Joey McLeister.*

During an evening with the intelligentsia in Petrozavodsk in 1986, news reporter Alexander "Sasha" Trubin of *Komsomolets* and I discussed journalism. We each had trouble understanding the other's way of doing business: the Russian newspaper did not report crime news or other negative information, so as not to frighten its readers, and the American newspaper changed size daily, depending on the number of advertisements. *Photograph by Joey McLeister.*

Petrozavodsk mayor Vladimir Dorchakov spoke no English, and I spoke no Russian, so it is not clear what we were trying to tell each other here, but whatever it was seemed to amuse and confound Tom Morgan *(center)*, who was fluent in both languages. *Photograph by Joey McLeister.*

During the initial sister-city visit to Petrozavodsk in 1986, Duluthians and former Americans gathered one evening in Mayme Sevander's apartment. *Left to right:* Saul Wagner, born in New York; Barb Hakala of Duluth; Ruth Niskanen, born in Palo, Minnesota; Laurie Hertzel of Duluth; Mayme Sevander, born in Superior, Wisconsin; Joyce Benson and Brooks Anderson, both of Duluth. *Back:* Mayme's daughter, Stella Sevander, is flanked by her husband, Igor Ryzhenkov, and by Mayme's brother, Paul Corgan. *Photograph by Joey McLeister.*

In Moscow in 1986, Tom Morgan, Joey McLeister, and I broke away from the tour group and had lunch on our own. The restaurants all served pretty much the same food, with little variety or choice: thin soup with noodles and a single meatball, cabbage salad, and fried meat patties topped with a fried egg. Salt cellars had no shaker tops, so to salt the food we dipped our fork handle into the salt and shook it over the plate. *Photograph by Joey McLeister.*

Copy editor Pamela Miller and printer John Fellbaum in the composing room on Miller's last night at the *News-Tribune* in 1986. The composing room was where the newspaper pages were pasted up late at night, with the news stories run through a hot-wax machine and then stuck onto full-sized sheets. Fellbaum's pocket displays some of the tools of his trade in the composing room: an X-Acto knife for cutting the type, a blue photo-invisible pen for marking copy, and a straightedge. Behind him on the peg board hang rolls of border tape and a roller for pressing it all firmly to the page. *Photograph by Igor Ryzhenkov.*

Elsa Mikkonen, who was born on Cape Cod, Massachusetts, was brought to the Soviet Union with her parents as a small girl and spent most of her life teaching English in the remote Russian village of Kotkozero, Karelia. She was one of a dozen American Finns I interviewed during my return trip to Petrozavodsk in 1991. She told me that she had been nervous about being interviewed by an American journalist, "but now I see that you are just a simple girl." *Photograph by Steven Stearns.*

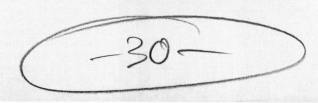

On June 9, 1994, I took part in my final *Duluth News-Tribune* news huddle, the afternoon meeting where the decisions for Page One are made. The next day, I left Duluth for a three-month fellowship in Columbus, Ohio, and then a new job in the Twin Cities. Photographer Steven Stearns shot this picture and scrawled –30– at the bottom, which, in newspaper tradition, means "the end" or "goodbye."

bands came from elsewhere to play at the Dreamland Ball-
room or the Arena-Auditorium. I had seen Gordon Light-
foot there myself just a few years before. So who needed the
Twin Cities? And who needed the *San Jose Mercury News*?
I refused to meet Murrell's eyes but glared off into the distance, trying fiercely not to cry.

"It's a real paper, Hertzbach," he said. "They have
bureaus all over the world. They have a whole bureau of
reporters in Washington, a whole newsroom there. Copy
editors have time—something we don't have here. You
work on two, maybe three stories all night. You have time
to really work it, time to ask questions, make it really good.
You'd love it."

I'd hate it, I thought. I had no interest in California, and
I had no idea what I would do with just two stories in an
eight-hour shift. I was used to running and gunning; I pictured myself editing the two stories in about half an hour
and then fidgeting for the rest of the night. I had no such
ambitions. Big newspapers are in big cities, and I was not
the least bit interested in a big city. I liked walking to work.
I liked the blustery, extreme weather of Duluth, the wild
areas, the bear that came around my backyard in the fall
and ate the sunflower seeds from my birdfeeder. I liked that
my dog could race leashless around the woods, and that the
woods were at the end of my street.

To celebrate his new job, Murrell bought a red Alfa
Romeo Spider convertible—"A California car," he said—and
we went for a drive up the North Shore. The car was so tiny
I could practically drag my fingertips on the ground when
I hung my arm out the window, and the stars were bright
enough to grab, hanging low over our heads. It was like

zooming up the Shore on a small motorized Barcalounger. *You won't have this in California,* I thought as we whizzed up the Scenic Highway toward Knife River, Lake Superior crashing on the rocks in the starry dark. *You will not have this kind of beauty and this kind of quiet.* I stubbornly refused to accept that in a bigger city, at a bigger paper, he might find something better. There could be nothing better than the woods and the lake and the intense, rugged seasons. Every Christmas for years, I sent him a card with the same plaintive message: Do you remember snow?

I spent four years on the regional desk. My beat was the Iron Range, primarily, but I also wrote about northern Wisconsin, Upper Michigan, and some of the communities up the North Shore—not the close-in towns, like Knife River and Two Harbors, but farther north: Lutsen, Grand Marais, Hovland—the far-flung, woodsy towns of Cook County. It was a great beat; there was always something going on, something controversial, newsy, or interesting. Once or twice a week, I would check out a staff car and head out to what we loosely called The Region to attend a council meeting, tour a taconite plant, interview a school superintendent. Most trips, I would also spend a couple of hours in someone's living room or kitchen, getting to know them for another kind of story, what newspapers call a human interest story. Though the Range was dotted with small towns that had started as mining locations a hundred years ago, I was surprised to find how few people actually lived in town. Most seemed to live miles out in the country, along forested rural roads in neat, newish ramblers, geraniums growing cheerfully in the front yard, the back garden fenced to keep out the deer. Space. People up there loved their space. While we talked, they would offer me what was known on the Range as "coffeeand"—a mug of strong black coffee and a plate of doughnuts, or cookies, or coffee cake.

These were the strong-minded children and grand-children of the immigrants who had settled the Range and worked the mines—Slavs, Serbs, Italians, Finns. Their parents and grandparents had left everything behind, sailed across the ocean, made their way to northern Minnesota, built sturdy houses with dovetail corners, and found jobs in the underground mine at Tower-Soudan, or the open-pit Hull-Rust-Mahoning mine near Hibbing, or at any of the scores of other mines scattered across the Mesabi, Vermilion, and Cuyuna ranges. They learned a new language; they built a life from the land and the trees. And it was almost as if the spirit of adventure and fortitude that drove them to the new world burned itself out in that generation; the Rangers that I met had no desire to roam, no desire to strike out for new places. They loved where they lived, deep in the woods, far from any big city. They followed their fathers into the mines; they bought pickup trucks and houses and boats; they spent their vacations hunting and fishing. When they traveled, if they traveled at all, it was usually back to the Old Country to visit ancient relatives; they showed me fading color photographs of frail elderly people in embroidered folk costumes, and of forests and lakes that were impossible to distinguish from the forests and lakes of northern Minnesota. They did not want to move to Duluth or Minneapolis, and they did not want the folks from the cities interfering with their way of life.

One snowy winter morning, I set off for Hibbing with

photographer Chuck Curtis to interview the superintendent of schools. Highway 53 to the Range was in pretty good shape, despite the heavy snow, but when we turned off onto 37 for the last half hour to Hibbing, the road was slippery. I slowed down, some. The little navy blue Citation staff car had automatic transmission and front-wheel drive, which I was not used to; I was used to the tepid Monza. A semi roared past, heading east, and it kicked up a cloud of snow. Still, I was not nervous. I had made this drive dozens of times, in all kinds of weather.

As we rounded a bend, the car began to slide, straight toward a water-filled ditch on the right-hand side of the road. Chuck, riding shotgun, didn't say a word. What happened next happened very quickly. I steered away from the ditch, but I overcorrected, and we slid across the oncoming lane of traffic, down into a ditch, and bumpity-bumpity-bumped into the woods. *Wham!* The car stopped with a jolt. I smacked my head on the steering wheel. Chuck banged his forehead on the rearview mirror before his seat belt yanked him back. And then all was quiet. We sat, stunned, and tried to assess the damage. The Citation had come to rest, somewhat miraculously, between two slender poplars. Through the windshield, I could see the crumpled hood of the car, from which steam was billowing. The thick wet snow continued to fall, making everything white and beautiful. Shame and embarrassment washed over me. How stupid could I be? I had clearly been going too fast, been too confident on these slippery roads. Just the week before, John Rott and I had driven to Washburn, Wisconsin, on snowy roads, and he had begged me to slow down. "I just got married," he said. "I don't want to make her a widow." And I had

....

laughed at him as I pressed the gas and zipped around an
icy curve. I thought I was skillful, but now it was clear that
I had only been lucky. Chuck mistook my silence for something worse. "Are you OK?" he asked.

"I'm fine," I said, but I still didn't move. I was too
ashamed.

"Are you sure? Are you in shock? Should I slap you?"

"You might want to slap me," I said. "But I'm not in
shock."

We climbed out of the Citation into the blowing snow.
Now what? We were miles from Hibbing, miles from anywhere. I crawled back into the car to get my purse and notebook; Chuck hauled out his camera bag. By some incredible
luck of timing, a state patrol car drove up. We waved and
struggled out of the slippery ditch. The patrolman rolled
down his window. "We went off the road," I said.

"Yeah, I see that," he said. "There's a convenience store
about a half mile back. You can call a wrecker from there."
And he rolled up the window and drove on. There was nothing else to do, then, but slide down the highway, our feet
soaked, the strap of the heavy camera bag digging into
Chuck's shoulder, to the 7-Eleven, where the clerk let us call
the newsroom. The welt on my forehead was getting big, so
he gave me a bag of frozen peas from the cooler to press
against my bruise. And there we sat, in the back of the store,
for more than two hours while reporter Carla Wheeler was
deployed to drive up and get us. Chuck was endlessly kind.
He did not criticize me for going off the road; instead, he
praised me for steering the car so skillfully between the
trees. (Right.) He chatted cheerfully with the store clerk
and made the story of our smashup sound funny instead

of irresponsible. Every now and then he wandered back to where I sat, frozen peas thawing against my throbbing head, to make sure I was really OK. He offered, again, to slap me. I just wearily shook my head.

By the time Carla arrived, the snow had stopped and the roads were only wet, which made me look even more foolish. *No, really, it was slippery a few hours ago!* We got back to the office by midafternoon, the interview with the school superintendent long forgotten. I am pretty sure that the dependable Krebs had called for me and canceled. Meanwhile, there were many things to live down, and eternal reminders of that snowy morning:

1. Forever after, Chuck referred to me as "Mario." As in Andretti.
2. The repaired Citation was never the same. It gained the nickname "the sidewinder."
3. You should see how slowly I drive in the snow now. I am not kidding. You could get there faster by dogsled.

Over time, I wrote hundreds of stories for the regional desk. None of them was terribly memorable, but looking back you can see a few constant themes, the biggest of which was change. Any story by itself is just that—a story, a moment in time. But taken together, good newspaper work should add up to something, many pieces of a larger picture, and in this case it added up to a significant shift in the way of life on the Iron Range, from prosperous and growing to much more hardscrabble.

Just like Duluth in the 1970s, the Iron Range had enjoyed boom times for years, with mines going great guns and offering full-time, lifelong employment. Range kids played hockey, worked in the mines and the taconite plants, rode snowmobiles in the winter, drove their big Chevy and Ford pickups when they went hunting and fishing. They loved it there with a fierce pride, and most of them assumed they would stay. This was God's country. This was the good life—as long as people from the Twin Cities didn't meddle. There were still tensions over recent environmental laws that prevented motor use in the Boundary Waters, prevented the logging of old-growth forests, and protected the timber wolf. One spring I drove to Ely and interviewed old Tommy Chosa, an Ojibwa wilderness guide who had lived in the woods up there his entire life. One March day he took his snowmobile from Ely to Basswood Lake in the BWCA to ice fish, and when he returned, the Forest Service ticketed him $100 for using a motor in a motors-free area. Chosa was a quiet, sensible guy but a determined one; he told me that as a Native American he and his people had rights that had been guaranteed by a treaty more than a hundred years before, and he was going to fight the ticket.

The Treaty of 1854 ceded thousands of acres of Native American land to the white man, but the Native Americans retained their right to hunt and fish, including in the BWCA. Chosa was looking forward to the fight. He knew that if he won, it would open the door for all kinds of other claims from Native Americans. He also knew that it was highly possible that the Forest Service would forgive his fine, just to keep things from getting noisy. And if they do, he told me with a grin, he would just have to take his snowmobile out there again.

Chosa's fight was only the beginning. Over the next few years, the Treaty of 1854 (and, in Wisconsin, treaties signed in 1837 and 1842) became the basis for argument that Native Americans should be allowed to spearfish and hunt outside of the white man's season. All three treaties had signed land over to the government but had preserved hunting and fishing rights. The backlash was, predictably, intense and often violent. In Wisconsin, especially, protesters showed up at boat landings when Native Americans went out to spearfish, sometimes throwing rocks and bottles, yelling, even shooting at the fishermen.

As the economy soured and the steel market grew glutted and the mines began laying off and closing, a lot of Rangers were forced to make a change. Politicians tried hard to bring in new industry, and they were always driving to the Range for a press conference to announce the possibilities of one thing or another, many of which never saw the light of day: a factory that was going to supply Asia with chopsticks, paper mills, mining reduction plants, and always, always the promise of something to do with Northwest Airlines—a reservation call center, or a maintenance facility, or something. Some of the ideas became reality, though seldom as impressive as first promised, and some simply evaporated for lack of funding. But nothing could replace the high-paying and abundant union jobs that had been lost.

As jobs vanished, towns shrank, and school districts consolidated, to great argument and fierce emotion. Lose a job? Yeah, that's bad. But merge your high school with the archrival high school down the road? That's a catastrophe. I covered endless school board meetings on this topic, recorded endless debates over which town's name would come first and which building would actually stay open. But it seemed that there was a larger story here, one that echoed what was going on in my own life, with my friends and colleagues: Everyone was moving to the Twin Cities.

Joey and I proposed a series of stories. Rangers were moving, but reluctantly. They loved where they lived, and the Cities, for the most part, didn't interest them. Most of those who did move, we found, were living in ratty trailer courts and flimsy apartment buildings in Blaine and Princeton and Anoka County, on the very northernmost edge of the Twin Cities, so they could make a fast getaway on the weekends back up north. They did not buy houses; they had houses, back in Hibbing and Virginia and Biwabik. They were not interested in moving into Minneapolis or St. Paul proper. They almost never went downtown. Once a year they held a big festive reunion at the Metrodome, all the Rangers in the Cities, together with a polka band and plenty of black coffee, hot dish, and potica. Governor Rudy Perpich, a Ranger himself, always showed up. They talked about who had married whom, and who was living where, and who had a job and who didn't, and mostly they talked about when they would be able to move back home.

I understood that pull, though it wasn't the Range that had my heart, but Duluth. When Joey and I drove around those northern Twin Cities suburbs, I shuddered at how complicated it was to get anywhere down in the Cities, how crowded it was, how built up and paved over. I made Joey do all the driving. In Duluth, the neighborhoods were studded with parks and woods and ravines. The North Shore was minutes away, and you didn't have to navigate eight-lane freeways when you came home again; you just glided back into town along leafy London Road, the lake glittering on your left. The worst thing you might encounter was a Monson truck rumbling past you up the highway. The steep hills of Duluth were slippery in the winter, but you were proud when you could get up them without sliding sideways, going slow and steady and never braking. I learned the unofficial Duluth rule of winter driving—yield to whoever is going up the hill, even if they have a stop sign and you don't. Besides, if the weather was really bad—or really nice— I could always leave my car behind and walk to work; it was only two miles. And, of course, there was the lake, wide and blue and cold. You could see it from just about anywhere in town, or hear the foghorn, or look up into the sky and watch the gulls wheeling and soaring overhead. In Anoka County, as Joey and I drove from trailer court to trailer court, all I could see was flat, and concrete, and cars. No hills, no lake, no foghorn, no ravines. Almost no trees—just miles and miles of headlights and taillights. I felt like I understood those displaced Iron Rangers as we finished our interviews and happily turned north.

I wrote a couple of stories about the Keewatin whistle, a piercing shriek that blew six times a day to call miners to their jobs. The local mine had long since closed, and some people complained that the whistle was now not only unnecessary but disruptive. One woman said that it woke her children, and she filed suit against the city asking that the whistle be turned off and that the city pay her $50,000. Others, of course, saw it as part of Keewatin's cultural heritage and wanted it to continue to blow, calling the ghosts of miners, perhaps, to their ghostly jobs. Keewatin was a small town, just a thousand residents, and it didn't have much else going on. That whistle helped define it. After yet another contentious city council meeting where people argued late into the night, a councilor stopped by as I tapped out my story on my bulky portable computer. "Your paper only comes up here when there's bad news," he snapped, and I looked at him in surprise. I hadn't seen the whistle story as bad news; I had seen it as interesting, another version of the End of an Era story. Still, he had a point; I was there because there was conflict. If they had simply turned the whistle off and no one had cared, there would be no story. News is, for the most part, tension—conflict between people, or between people and government, or between governments, if you want to think really big and think about war. Over time, my goal became to find stories that were not necessarily negative but had texture. I loved the thrill of breaking news as much as any reporter, but I did not get jazzed about policy stories and meeting stories and political wrangling the way many of my colleagues did. I was interested in tales, and I began to think of myself more broadly—not just as a journalist but as a storyteller.

I realized pretty early that I was drawn to stories about people who would not normally be in the newspaper. Some would call these feature stories, but in my mind there was a distinction between features (which I considered to be fluffy, "nice" stories) and what I was trying to do. I wanted to tell tales about real life—how real people handled change and obstacles and tragedies and successes. Like Sue Willoughby writing about the homeless guys on First Street, like Jacqui Banaszynski telling the story of Harmon Seaver, like Ruth Hammond writing about the woman who lived in the haunted house under the Blatnik Bridge.

I had read many stories like these on the wires during

my four years on the copy desk, and I was pretty sure I could do it myself. I just had to find them. Krebs was a good editor for that. He gave me his share of filler and fluff assignments (the newspaper came out every day, after all, and we had to feed the beast), but he also had an eye for newsy features, stories that showed how news events affected people's lives. These stories gave me glimpses into the many ways that people lived. I was amazed to see how much variety there was, even in this one small part of the world, how many different beliefs there were, and philosophies, and experiences. The Range had entrepreneurs and rednecks and socialists and farmers and hippies and born-agains; people were attracted to the remote northern woods for a whole variety of reasons. I thought I knew something of the history of the region—the Seven Iron Men, Gus Hall, the blackballing of Finns during the strikes of the 1920s—but I came to realize that I knew next to nothing, really, about the heritage of northern Minnesota, and if I was going to be able to write intelligent stories, I had better learn quick. I had grown up in Duluth's East End in an insular family that was big enough to be its own society and thought it had everything figured out. But you cannot approach journalism with the idea that you have everything figured out; you have to approach stories, and people, with a very open mind, lest you run the risk of not hearing what it is they have to say. Journalism, I was coming to see, even though it was small-city journalism, was broadening my worldview.

My father sometimes called me up with his critiques, which were usually ambiguous. "It's remarkable that you can write so quickly and yet with so much authority," he said, more than once. "When I write an article, I sometimes get lost in the material. But you never do." I decided to take that as a compliment, but I wasn't entirely sure.

One May, Joey and I drove to Shell Lake, Wisconsin, to interview a woman who was facing charges of practicing midwifery without a license. It was a beautiful spring day, the leaves yellow green and tiny, as we headed south down Highway 53. Leigh Lawson was a calm, thoughtful woman who had given birth twice at home and who had made it her life mission to help other women have their babies at home if they so chose. If there was a complication, she didn't hesitate to call the paramedics. And that was what got her in trouble; she assisted in the birth of a baby who had trouble breathing, and she called 911. The parents were not the ones who filed the complaint; it was the ambulance attendants. Lawson was eventually found innocent, and Joey and I had great plans to go back and be there for a home birth and do a big Sunday story, but we never did; we had moved on to the next story, and the next.

I wrote about the first person in northern Minnesota to die of AIDS, and how his friends and family shunned him at the end, terrified that they, too, would contract the disease. "People are panicking," the man's friend said. I wrote about one of the first families to legally homeschool their children once the legislature changed the law; their house outside of Grand Rapids was so remote that on my way to visit them a black bear waddled across the highway in front of my car. I wrote about people who were coping with strange, powerful conditions—agoraphobia, and fibromyalgia, and chronic fatigue syndrome. Bob Allen and I teamed up to write a series of stories about gays in the northland; this was the early 1980s, and most of them refused to be quoted by name for fear their houses would be burned, or they would lose their jobs, or their families would be attacked. I wrote a series of stories about the ways that people's lives change once they've grown old, becoming widows, or caregivers, or victims of Alzheimer's; living in nursing homes or senior high-rise apartments where the old people walk out every day to McDonald's for a cup of coffee, until something happens—a fall, an illness—and suddenly one of them can't.

Some of the other reporters took to calling me the Sob Sister. And I suppose I was, in a way. My goal, though, was not to make people cry; it was to illustrate for readers the many different ways of living, to show them how many different kinds of people and lives there were, right there in northern Minnesota. It helped, I think, that every story I wrote was eye-opening to me. I could prowl around and poke into people's lives, look inside their homes, ask them all kinds of questions. The best advice I got was from another reporter who told me to never be afraid of looking stupid. "Ask everything," he said. "Ask stuff even if you think you already know the answer." I did, and it turned out that the answer was seldom what I had assumed. I had gone into this job a shy, somewhat sheltered young woman from the nice part of town. But now I was learning about nuance and about life. Through telling these stories, I began to see both the possibilities and the limitations of daily journalism, and I was beginning to see that there was more to the world than news.

My workweek started with a Monday night general assignment shift. I came in at 2:00 P.M. and walked across the street to the police station to look through the bookings, and then I covered night meetings that beat report-

ers couldn't get to, or made calls to round out unfinished
stories written by daysiders. I loved the GA assignment
because you never knew what was going to get thrown your
way. Part of the job involved doing the checks—calling all
the sheriff's departments and cop shops and state patrol
dispatchers from Duluth to the Canadian border, and from
Grand Rapids, Minnesota, all the way to Ironton, Michigan,
looking for news. Most nights, it was tedious work, just one
unfruitful phone call after another. "Pretty quiet," the dispatcher would usually say, even if you could hear sirens
screaming on the other end of the phone. ("It's nothing.")
But every once in a while you would get a good story, like
the time when days of heavy rain caused a hillside up the
North Shore to suddenly give way; tons of rocks and mud
slid across Highway 61 one evening, dragging trees and
boulders and a semitruck right off the road and down the
hill toward the lake.

I got the name of the trucker from the state patrol and
spent a couple of hours calling and leaving messages everywhere I could think of. Just before deadline, he called me
back. "My wife says you're looking for me," he said, and then
gave me a matter-of-fact but fascinating interview. He had
not been hurt, and even though his truck had tipped over
and his trailer had ripped in half, he said he had not been
very rattled. He just rode the mudslide down the hill, "like a
surfboard," he said.

The best stories, though, usually came out of Wisconsin. That had been true back in the copy desk days when
I had sorted the state and Wisconsin wires, and that was
true now that I was responsible for the regional cop checks.
One night the dispatcher told me about a widow from

Hurley named Julia Cornetto who had been burglarized, and I gave her a call. Julia turned out to be a great talker. She told me that she had heard someone in her house late one night. "It was about three in the morning," she said. "I've got wind chimes hanging on the porch, and I was wondering why they were ringing so hard. Then I thought I heard a little noise downstairs. Your hair goes up, and your back gets like an icicle. I tiptoed to the top of the stairs, and there, dear God, there was this man in my house."

She slipped back into her bedroom and picked up the first thing she saw—the large plastic crucifix that she kept on the neat, narrow bed of her late husband. Crucifix in hand, she crept up behind the burglar and started whaling him on the head with it. *Wham! Wham! Wham!* She told me that the plastic cross splintered, but the metal body of Christ remained whole. "He was holding his head, saying, 'Stop it! Stop it! You're hurting me! Stop it this minute!' I kept beating him."

The burglar ran outside, where the cops found him bleeding in the snow. I worked hard at the story, making it as entertaining as I could, but the copy desk outshone me with their perfect headline: Woman Uses Right Cross to Batter a Burglar.

I drove to Grand Marais many times to cover endless meetings about the impending closure of the elementary school in Tofte. Most of Cook County is public land; the tax base is very small, and the few residents are scattered over a large area. The county could no longer afford to keep two elementary schools open, but closing Birch Grove meant the kids at the south end of the county would have to ride the school bus for more than an hour twice a day. In the winter, this meant riding in the frigid dark, both there and back.

I liked covering these meetings; it was an interesting story, and you could easily see all sides—the financial conundrum as well as the human toll. I lugged along a heavy portable computer and wrote my story in a quiet classroom after the meeting had ended. The computer had a long patch cord with couplers on one end, which I attached to the earpiece and mouthpiece of a telephone in order to transmit my story to the computer back in the newsroom. Sometimes I could borrow the superintendent's phone, but I always brought a few quarters with me in case I had to use the pay phone. That was more difficult, because the patch cord to the couplers was pretty short and I had to sort of hoist up the computer and hold it there while the story transmitted. It was cumbersome, but it usually worked. And if it didn't, I just called the city desk and asked, "Can someone take dictation?"

And then there was nothing more to do except drive home, an hour and a half down Highway 61 in the black night through Little Marais and Beaver Bay and Silver Bay and Castle Danger, on down to Duluth, listening to a radio station from the Upper Peninsula that beamed clearly across Lake Superior. There were always deer on those trips back, and you had to be careful; one night I counted more than eighty along the side of the road, their eyes glowing yellow in the dark.

One summer, John Rott and I drove up to Mountain Iron to spend a day with Pete Hawkins, a miner with U.S. Steel's Minntac plant who was out of work because of what was either a strike or a lockout—it depended on who you were talking to. I had already written about the larger ramifications of the dispute and given the official points of view of the company and the union. But what about the human side? What did it do to a person's life to be without work in this way? How did a miner spend his days when he couldn't work? Where did money come from? What were his worries? How did he live? Rott and I didn't have a lot of time for context or perspective; all we had time for was one guy's view. I hoped we had chosen the right guy. We drove up to the Range early on a Thursday morning, spent time with Pete walking the picket line, buying groceries, helping his wife make dinner, lamenting that he didn't have enough money to take his two-year-old son to Dairy Queen. We drove back to Duluth late that night. I wrote the story on Friday, and it ran on Sunday. That's how it went in those days—you did everything fast, and then you went on to something else.

My father read the story in the Sunday paper and called me up. "It was an interesting story," he allowed. "But one word bothered me." One word, out of two thousand? "You wrote—" and I could hear the rustle of the newspaper as he folded the section, looking for the line. "You wrote, 'His tennies left flat tracks in the wet grass,'" my father read. "Tennies? This is a big guy. Tennies are something a little kid wears. I don't think that's the word you were looking for. This guy didn't wear tennies." One word out of two thousand. It haunted me. He was right. Word choice was important, and even on deadline, even when I was writing hundreds of words, I needed to pay attention to precision of language. "Use the right word, not its second cousin," Mark Twain said. I had always liked that and quoted it rather freely, but now I decided to actually pay attention to it myself. I wrote it down and taped it to the side of my computer monitor.

Some of the newer reporters who had gone to J school counseled me as I learned on the job; Katy Read, the features writer, suggested that my stories could use more context. She helped me see that while telling one story intimately could make it powerful, broadening it with perspective from experts could give it meaning. Hmmmm. This had not occurred to me, nor had any of my editors ever mentioned it. It was clear that things were done so fast in the newsroom—stories assigned, reported, written, slammed into the paper—that any improvement would happen on our own. The art of interviewing I learned from Georgia Swing, shamelessly eavesdropping on her telephone calls. She sat across from me for a couple of years before moving over to the city desk. She was polite, clear, direct, and absolutely persistent. I used to listen to her interviews with admiration; even not hearing their answers, I could tell she was not letting people get away with much. She would repeat the question; she would point out politely but firmly that the question had not yet been answered; she never got mad or impatient; she would just ask it again. She would say, quite frankly and without a hint of embarrassment, "I don't understand," when they tried to snow her. You just knew that, unlike that reporter I had copyedited years before, Georgia would never write a peat story that she didn't fully understand.

It was Georgia's husband, Virgil, who gave me tips for face-to-face interviews. We seldom used tape recorders, and you had to scribble very fast to get everything down. "Come up with your own shorthand," Virgil said. "Be consistent, so you know what your abbreviations mean." He also suggested writing questions on the inside cover of the notebook, flipping back during the interview to make sure you've covered the ground you want. Follow the direction the interview takes you; there might be surprising stuff you would miss if you stuck only to your scripted questions. If they say something brilliant and you want to get an exact quote, ask a throwaway question, something to keep them talking while you continue to write down the previous answer. And always end the interview with two questions: One, ask if there was something you should have asked, but didn't. And two, ask if it's OK to call back with follow-up questions. Because you'll almost always think of something later.

Oh, and the best advice? Take along a Flair pen, or a pencil, for outdoor interviews in the winter. Ink pens tend to freeze.

Because I wrote tales, I gathered as much ambience as I could when I was on interviews. But sometimes when I called back for more information, it was to ask questions that sources thought a bit bizarre: What color are your eyes? What color was the shirt you were wearing when I interviewed you—was it green, or blue? Do you happen to remember what song was playing on the radio? Details, details—the power of storytelling lies in the details, and even though I tried to take note of everything, once I started writing the story I almost always realized there was some key thing that I had forgotten to record.

One day, Larry Fortner stopped by my desk. He was puffing thoughtfully on his pipe, which usually meant that he had a good idea. "There's an old fisherman north of Grand Marais who I hear is planning a traditional Viking funeral," he said. I had no idea what a traditional Viking funeral was, but I knew better than to turn down the possibility of a summer road trip up the North Shore. "I'm there," I said.

The old fisherman's name was Helmer Aakvik. He lived in a small house on the rocky shore of Lake Superior just outside of Hovland, about two and a half hours north of Duluth. John Rott and I checked out a staff car and headed north. The drive up was gorgeous, hugging the rocky shore past Grand Marais, nearly all the way to the Canadian border, and while Rott drove, I looked out at the crashing waves and the gulls gliding above them. There was no other place in the world I wanted to be.

Hovland is tiny—just a scattering of houses, a shop that sells deer-hide mittens, a post office, and a Norwegian Lutheran church. It is hemmed on one side by the pine forests of the Sawtooth Mountains, and on the other side by the lake. We turned down the steep dirt road that led to the Aakvik house, just feet from the water's edge. Driving into the yard was like going back in time. An elderly woman in a long, dark skirt and a head scarf came up to greet us: Christine Aakvik, his wife. An old guy sat out in the yard mending nets; he had a lined face stubbled with white and a mouth that looked downturned in a permanent scowl, though he was not unfriendly, just quiet. Though the weather was warm, his creased shirt was buttoned up to his Adam's apple, and the sleeves came down to his knobby wrists. He was sitting on the rocks, unsnarling the knots from a fishing net with swollen fingers: Helmer.

By now I had done a little research, enough to know that Helmer Aakvik was legendary in North Shore history, as a fisherman and a pioneer, and a courageous man. He was nearing ninety, but he was still sharp, and he looked at

Rott and me with bemusement. He didn't say much. We followed him inside. The house was small and crammed with stuff—piles of magazines and newspapers stacked on the floors with just a pathway to walk through, way too much furniture, and geraniums perched on shelves, dimming the light from the windows. We threaded single file through the hallway to the crowded sitting room. "So," I said, in my best important reporter voice as we settled in our chairs. "I hear you are planning a traditional Viking funeral."

"A what?" Aakvik said.

"A Viking funeral. You know, having someone set you on fire and float you out to sea." It sounded preposterous as I said it out loud. Aakvik sat back in his chair and looked at me. And then he chuckled. "I can't do that," he said. "That would be illegal."

We stared at each other in silence. After a while, Helmer started talking. He told us about the old days on Lake Superior, when herring and trout could be hauled in by the netful and Hovland was nothing more than a couple of fishing shacks. He told us the story of his daring attempt to rescue a young, inept fisherman in the icy waters of Lake Superior during a fierce storm. All day and all night, Aakvik was alone on his boat, riding the waves, fighting to stay awake, chopping the ice off his motor with a hatchet, soaked to the skin, searching, in vain, for the young man.

He told us how much things up the Shore had changed, and how the fishing industry had changed. And now his fishing days were just about over. He told us that he had commissioned someone to build his coffin—it was out in his shed, even now, if we would like to see it. Rott and I looked at each other. Why, yes, we would.

The coffin in his shed was a beautiful long wooden box, fitted with a flat lid engraved with a curious design. I ran my hand over the lid; it was smooth and strong, sanded to silk. At one end, the carpenter had engraved the name, AAKVIK. And underneath that, a compass rose. Rott and I asked why. Helmer squinted at us in the bright summer sun, and when he spoke, his Norwegian accent made his words pure poetry. "It's so after I'm gone, I can navigate among the moon and the stars."

•

Reporting from Russia

....

CHRIS ISON WAS OTHERWISE OCCUPIED—COVERING
city hall, exposing corruption, bringing down the mayor—
so I slipped in and took the Russia assignment away from
him. Or maybe I didn't; maybe he wasn't interested. He had
written the initial story, just an ordinary city council report
about Duluth wanting a sister city in the Soviet Union. But
after that he got busy with other things, and somehow the
story bounced to me.

Ison had black hair and a scruffy goatee and a dry sense
of humor. We were great friends and occasional drinking
buddies, and we used to fight about whose stories belonged
on Page One—his hard-nosed, hard-news important stuff,
or my slice-of-life Sob Sister pieces. (Answer: both. And
then we would have another beer.) Larry Fortner had hired
him in 1983 right out of college to cover the city of Superior. Ison was a master interviewer; he knew that reporters
who play dumb get much better stuff than reporters who
swagger around and act like they already know everything.
He was so good at this that sources often found themselves
patiently walking him through just about anything and telling him much more than they had ever intended. It was a
beautiful thing to behold, and since my desk was near his
and I could easily eavesdrop on his phone interviews, I

had the pleasure of beholding it fairly often. Ison believed strongly in the watchdog role of newspapers and one summer decided to check up on our elected officials by calling their offices on Friday afternoons to see who was around and who had slipped out early. Several of us were enlisted to help with this assignment, and sunny Friday after sunny Friday I called city managers, only to find that everyone was at work, nobody had taken off, and Ison had no story. "That's so Minnesota," he grumbled.

The Superior cops nicknamed him "Columbo," as much for his trench coat as for his disarming habit of shooting the breeze in a low-key, friendly way and then turning back and zinging them with just one more question. After stirring things up in Superior—he wrote about the city council's inappropriate habit of holding closed-door sessions to discuss city business, and he also got the paper to sue the police department for withholding crime reports—he moved over to cover Duluth City Hall, where he wrote a series of investigative pieces that led to the indictment of the mayor. (Eventually, the mayor, John Fedo, was acquitted and served out his term, but by then Ison had moved on to the *Star Tribune* in the Twin Cities.)

So a little thing like a sister-city relationship wasn't of much interest to him. It wasn't of much interest to me, either, at first; I saw it as a largely symbolic gesture, like a resolution proclaiming a town to be a nuclear-free zone. But after I started covering the story, I quickly found out that the mission of the sister-city group was neither meaningless nor purely symbolic. It was literal, and it was sincere; the group really did want to establish an active friendship with a city in the Soviet Union. They had one all picked out and ready to go—Petrozavodsk, the capital of the Soviet republic of Karelia in northern Russia, near the Finnish border. But the Soviet Union had not approved an American sister-city friendship since 1973, thirteen years before, and the Duluth group received no clear answer to its persistent letters and telexes. If they were discouraged, their leader, a mild-mannered, bearded minister named Brooks Anderson, was not. Brooks simply did not see obstacles where other people did. If Russia wouldn't respond to Duluth, he said, then Duluth would just . . . show up. A trip was scheduled for late August 1986. The delegation made plans to fly from Duluth to Chicago to Belgrade to Moscow (that last leg a four-hour flight on Yugo Air), take the train to Leningrad, take an overnight train to Petrozavodsk, and then, weary, exhausted, rumpled, and wrinkled, present themselves to the mayor of Petrozavodsk, en masse, and politely ask, "Will you be our sister?"

Now *this* was a story. I went to Larry Fortner. "We have to go," I said. "You have to send me to Russia." I knew that this was an audacious suggestion; the *Duluth News-Tribune* seldom sent anyone anywhere, except for the Iron Range; other than when the legislature was in session, we rarely even sent reporters to the Twin Cities. My request to go to the Soviet Union was so preposterous as to be laughable, but it was such a good story that I couldn't give up. The sister-city group was an eclectic blend of people—not just idealists like Brooks but politicians, teachers, ministers, professors, business owners, and students. And Petrozavodsk was an interesting choice. The group had not picked it at random; they had looked for a Soviet city that was similar to Duluth. And like Duluth, Petrozavodsk sat on the

edge of a big lake. Like Duluth, it was surrounded by pine
and birch forests, and its economy depended on lumbering,
shipping, and tourism. Many Finns and Finnish-speaking
people lived there; until the Winter War of 1939, when the
USSR annexed miles of Finnish land and displaced half a
million people, primarily in Karolia, Petrozavodsk had been
much closer to the Finnish border than it was now.

The other connections were less well known. During
the Great Depression, thousands of idealistic American
Finns had sold their homes and farms and moved to the
Soviet Union, heeding Lenin's invitation for workers of the
world to unite and help build communism. Many ended up
in Petrozavodsk or other small towns in Karelia. The phe-
nomenon was called Karelian Fever, and some said that
the Finns had been coerced, or even tricked. Few of them
had ever come back. I interviewed a Duluth doctor named
Erkki Leppo who was deeply opposed to the choice of Petrozavodsk for this reason. Leppo had served in the Finnish
army, and he had worked in Petrozavodsk. His memories
of the Winter War were still vivid, and he remembered the
Soviets hunkering down in Petrozavodsk as they planned
to invade his country. His mother-in-law was buried in a
cemetery that had once been on Finnish soil but, since the
Winter War, was now Russian. Leppo made it very clear to
me that he did not oppose the idea of a Soviet sister city
in theory, but he thought Petrozavodsk's history was too
tragic for Finns, especially for local Finns. I listened to his
concerns, and I wrote a story about them, but I fear I did
not give him the credence I should have. I was twenty-nine
years old and had scarcely been outside of Minnesota; to
me, World War II was ancient history, and Stalin's purges

were remote, another world, another lifetime away. In my foolish mind, these things had little to do with this bright group of well-meaning Duluthians who were eager to go to the Soviet Union—the Evil Empire, as Ronald Reagan called it then—and make friends.

I went back to Fortner. "It's only $1,200," I said. "For everything. Airfare, food, hotels, everything. You could barely send me to New York for that amount."

"We wouldn't send you to New York anyway," Fortner said, puffing on his pipe. He said he would think about it. Keep covering their meetings, he told me. And I did, on my own time, in the evenings, listening as their plans took shape, hearing their descriptions of what they hoped to do, getting more and more jazzed. I called Joey, who had left the paper and was now freelancing in the Twin Cities, and I told her about the trip, and she got jazzed too. Finally, along about midsummer, the group reached a point where they needed a firm head count. They asked for a deposit of $100 from each person. Joey immediately sent in her check; if I was going, she was going, too, to photograph the journey. All of this was good news; now Fortner had to make a decision. I went back to him. "I need a hundred dollars to reserve a spot," I said. But Fortner was wily. "I'll approve the hundred," he said, and just as I was giving a triumphant little fist clench, he added, "But that doesn't mean you're necessarily going."

But in the end, I did go. I kept attending meetings and writing stories and chipping away at the arrangements, and on August 28, 1986, my parents drove me to the Duluth airport, where I, lugging a duffle bag full of pocket-sized notebooks, my old high school Nikkormat camera, not enough

film, and too many ballpoint pens, boarded the plane for
Minneapolis with a crushing headache and a mix of dread
and excitement in the pit of my stomach. I had $200 cash
in the zippered pocket of my little embroidered purse and
several fistfuls of crossed-flag lapel pins—the American and
Soviet flags—to give as gifts. Fortner had never said yes to
the trip, but he had never said no. And I figured I would live
by the adage "It's easier to seek forgiveness than permission."

We landed in Moscow at 4:00 A.M. on Saturday, August 30,
1986, though our weary, jetlagged bodies thought it was
7:00 P.M. Friday. We had not slept since Wednesday, save
for whatever stiff-necked zzzs we had managed to grab
on the crowded and stuffy airplane; we had spent seven
hours in Yugoslavia, but with nowhere to nap we roamed
Belgrade's farmers' market and picked through souvenirs
left over from the Sarajevo Olympics. Joey and I poked our
heads into a Serbian Orthodox church and emerged dazzled
and woozy from the icons and incense. Our group recon-
vened for dinner at an ancient restaurant called Two Deer,
and then, at midnight, we boarded the plane for Russia.

The Moscow airport was quiet before dawn, and we
were beyond exhausted; the low ceiling pressed toward our
heads as we stumbled through the dim terminal. The border guards did not smile, did not welcome us to the Soviet
Union. They looked down on us from their elevated glassed-
in booths, checking our passports, asking the occasional
sharp question that we tried, clumsily, in our jetlagged state,
to understand. We did our best to look like friendly Americans, not a spy among us. My eyes felt like sandpaper, my

knees were trembling from fatigue, and I wondered if my matted and frizzy hair, thirty-six hours uncombed, looked anything close to the picture on my passport. Would they let me in? Somewhere in the airport, a baby wailed. "That's how I feel," someone said, and we all laughed uncertainly. Was it OK to laugh? After staggering through customs, we waited three hours for the Intourist bus to arrive to take us to our hotel, slumped on the terminal floor in a state of half wake, half sleep. Brooks pulled out his video camera. "I think we should record this dreary moment," he said. "It's a mean, ugly mood."

My assignment on this trip was twofold: to record the sister-city negotiations and to give readers a flavor of ordinary life behind the Iron Curtain. Once we reached Petrozavodsk, Fortner expected me to call the newsroom every evening and file a story for the next day. The paper had made much of my assignment, advancing the coverage with house ads and ginning up a logo: "Report from Russia," with a line drawing of a Petrozavodsk onion-dome church and Duluth's Aerial Bridge. But we would not be in Petrozavodsk for several days yet; the itinerary, set down by Intourist in its immutable way, called for two nights in Moscow and then three full days in Leningrad. Our schedule was tightly controlled, hour by hour—guided tours of the palatial Moscow subways, bus tours of both cities, visits to the Hermitage and to berioska shops, those hard-currency boutiques where tourists stock up on nesting dolls, icons, and flowered scarves. I was expected to find stories about the Russian people, not stories about thirty-three Duluthians riding the Intourist bus and buying lacquered boxes, so Joey and I made arrangements with one of the delegation members

to slip away and explore Moscow and Leningrad on our
own. Tom Morgan was the marketing director at the *News-
Tribune*, though he was not on this trip as a representative
of the newspaper; he held a doctorate in Russian language
and literature and had been to the Soviet Union twice before
and had come along because of his deep personal interest.
He was a cheerful, easygoing guy who wore a bow tie, and
since he was fluent in the language and familiar with the
geography, Joey and I figured he would be an ideal companion. The trick, of course, was to avoid getting herded
onto that omnipresent red tourist bus. So every morning,
we sneaked back to our rooms after breakfast and waited
until the bus had pulled away. Our Intourist guide, Masha
Zhuravleva (who many of the Duluthians insisted on calling "Marsha"), waited as long as she could, tapping her foot,
checking her watch, knowing that some of us were missing,
but eventually we would see the bus drive off, and then Joey,
Tom, and I would regroup and set out to explore on our own.

I did not know what to expect. To prepare for this trip,
I had interviewed people who had been to the USSR, I read
Hedrick Smith's book *The Russians*, and, on Tom's recom-
mendation, I reread *Anna Karenina*. ("That book will tell
you all you need to know about Russia," he said, and perhaps that was true, but it did not tell me all I needed to know
about the Soviet Union.) I was still shockingly ignorant. I
had no idea what being there would be like. Would we be
watched? Followed? Stopped? If I tried to take a picture of a
bridge or a soldier, would someone from the KGB step over
solemnly and rip the film from my camera? Would anybody
talk to us? If they did, would they tell us the truth? Tom,
however, was almost giddy, happy to be there again, and

the three of us set off to find to some of his favorite places (though we never fulfilled his often-stated desire to eat ice cream in Gorky Park). Moscow was busy, with wide streets and gray buildings that looked older and more decrepit than they should have looked. People hurried past, some quite sophisticated, others dressed in clothes that I could only describe as peculiar: baseball caps and aprons on thick-set elderly women. Beautiful flowered scarves draped across the shoulders of young women; the same scarves were pulled tightly over the heads of elderly women and knotted under the chin. The lack of consumer goods was evident in details: the exact same shade of pink lipstick on many women I passed. I found myself staring at the faces, inward turned and inscrutable. Not many met my eyes. None returned my tentative and open American smile. As they walked, heads down, men in wrinkled trousers spat on the sidewalk and kept going. A few beige Ladas zipped to and fro, and lumbering buses spewed smoky, black exhaust. Stocky women swept the streets with straw brooms. Industrial gray machines on the street corners dispensed mineral water and a mildly fermented drink called kvass for a few kopecks; everyone used the same glass, which was cleaned between customers with a hasty rinse. Germs be damned; I gave it a try, glugging the yeasty drink and rinsing the glass for the man behind me. And the lines! Everywhere, people lined up. Sometimes they would see a line forming and join it, not knowing for sure what there was to purchase at the other end. But it was better to save your place first, and then determine if you wanted whatever was being sold. Inside a department store, we watched a line snake through the aisles and up the stairs, everyone waiting to buy wallpaper.

Down a sidewalk and around a corner, another line, waiting to buy watermelons from a man in a hat seated at a wooden table with a scale and an abacus.

I joined a long line that ended at a truck, where two men were selling ice-cream cones. The cones had been made in advance and packed into cartons unwrapped; each just had a film of plastic pressed over the top to prevent drips. The woman in front of me opened her handbag and neatly filled it with a dozen cones, and I despaired that she would buy them all. But as she tucked away the last one, one of the guys reached into the back of the truck, pulled out another cardboard carton, slit it open, and began handing out more cones.

I peeled the film off my ice cream as I rejoined Tom and Joey, who were standing under a propaganda billboard that showed enormous happy workers smiling as they emerged from factories, biceps bulging, clutching hammers. Tom translated the vibrant slogans, which were spelled out in what looked like backward letters: THE IDEAS OF LENIN LIVE AND WILL BE VICTORIOUS! THE POLITICS OF THE COMMUNIST PARTY OF THE SOVIET UNION ARE THE POLITICS OF PEACE! THE WORKING CLASS WILL NOT BE DAUNTED! We walked past bus stops, where *Pravda* was tacked up each morning on wooden notice boards for commuters to read while they waited. I stopped and examined the newspaper—it looked old-fashioned, with no pictures or ads at all. No ads? Of course; there was no need to advertise. This was the Soviet Union, where there was ostensibly no private commerce. (So who was selling the ice cream?)

Avoiding the bus tours meant that Joey and I missed seeing many of the splendors of Russia. Somehow, I figured we would be back; we would have a chance later. But we did not. I did not see the magnificent Moscow subways, with their great art and massive glittering chandeliers. I did not stand in line to view Lenin's body. I am not quite sure if I even made it to Red Square, if I ever glimpsed St. Basil's Cathedral or the Kremlin; if I did, I didn't have time to go inside. Instead, I was at Detsky Mir, buying toys. Detsky Mir—Children's World—was a cavernous Moscow store that was not so much a world filled with toys as it was a world sparsely scattered with them. Glass showcases had been placed every few feet, with a few odd playthings in each one. The display cases were locked, and customers were not allowed to touch the merchandise. Instead, you had to find a clerk, point to what you wanted, and wait while she retrieved the items for you. (Though of course if you spoke Russian you didn't have to point; you could speak.) The toys were then handed to another employee, who wrapped them in coarse gray paper. Then you were directed to yet another employee, who toted up the cost on an abacus. I stared at her quick fingers as she clickety-clicked the black beads back and forth on their wires, coming up with a total, which she wrote down on a slip of paper. This I presented to the cashier. She took my rubles and handed me another slip of paper, which I brought to the woman who held my packages. I gave her the receipt, and she gave me my purchases—a set of toy metal cars, and a miniature abacus. All of these women were standing behind a glass counter, a few feet apart. They did not speak. They did not try to consolidate their duties. They each had a task to do, and they did it. This was full employment, Soviet style.

As we walked the streets of Moscow, Tom stopped

people and struck up easy conversations. We talked to old
soldiers whose jacket lapels sparkled with pins commemo-
rating their service in World War II; one of them, a gray-
bearded man named Alexander, had once held a job writing
slogans for those propaganda billboards. The Great Patri-
otic War, as they called it, was very close in his memory,
and he tried to impress on us how much Russia had suffered, and how much his country valued peace. He had lived
through the siege of Leningrad, he said. He did not want to
see another war.

On Sunday, Tom, Joey, and I accompanied some of the
Duluthians to services at a Baptist church, the only active
Protestant church in Moscow. The brick building was plain
enough on the outside, and I mistook it for an apartment
complex, but inside were tall arched windows, sparkling
crystal chandeliers, and a balcony packed with fervent wor-
shipers. The minister, Anatoly Sokolov, told us that Richard
Nixon had visited in 1972 and Billy Graham had preached
there in 1982, so if now, in 1986, we were thinking that we
had discovered a group of underground Christians hud-
dling in fear, we were mistaken. One of the Duluthians, the
Reverend Thomas Little, had hoped to preach while in Russia, and he asked Sokolov if he could deliver a sermon, but
Sokolov gently turned him down; Little had to be satisfied
with posing for pictures later, at the altar, after the worship-
ers had gone home.

After two days, the sister-city group packed up and
moved to Leningrad, where Joey, Tom, and I continued to
duck out in the mornings and make our own way through
the city. At the Hermitage we sat outside, talking with a
Russian man who asked us to buy him vodka. He said he

liked to hang around tourist attractions so he could practice his English with visitors, but I suspected he was more
interested in the vodka. Joey and I finally slipped into the
museum, but we were able to tour only one room before a
babushka came up and indicated that it was closing for the
day. The Hermitage! We went all the way to Leningrad and
didn't see the Hermitage! Instead, we walked to the Admi-
ralty Bar and talked to three young Russians who were having one last drink before heading out for their mandatory
month of harvesting potatoes on a communal farm. The
young woman in the group wore a bright purple sweater
and had long polished nails. All three were drinking cham-
pagne and eating appetizers, and none of them looked
happy about how they would be spending their September.

The next afternoon, Tom and I went to the Museum of
the History of Religion and Atheism, which was in the former Kazan Cathedral, a Russian Orthodox church on Leningrad's main street of Nevsky Prospekt. Two long wings
curved out from either side of a central dome; the building
was modeled after St. Peter's Basilica in Rome but now was
filled with religious art presented in a historical, rather than
spiritual, context. We wandered through displays of arti-
facts; at one point I leaned in close to get a better look at a
spiked whip used by certain sects for self-flagellation, when
one of the museum babushkas—there was one in every
room, keeping a sharp eye on us—appeared at my side and
began hollering at me in Russian. She was a tiny woman in
black stockings and slippers, but she was ferociously angry,
or so she sounded. I looked at her, bewildered, and Tom
came to my rescue. "Don't lean on the glass," he said, and
he apologized in Russian to the glowering woman. Then he

turned to me. "I told her you were an ignorant American," he said. The babushka did not look mollified.

"Let's find the gift shop," I said.

The museum gift shop turned out to be nothing more than a table set up along a dim side hall; a few postcards were on display, and not much else, but I was interested in the poster that hung behind it on the wall, which showed a black-and-white line drawing of the building and the museum name in Russian. Tom asked the price, and the man at the table glanced up and down the hall and then spoke quickly. "We need to come back tomorrow at two, to the side door," Tom told me. "He wants us to bring him the name and address of an American pen pal." We had those aplenty, pressed upon us by Duluthians before we left. So the next day, just an hour or two before heading to the train station, we showed up at the museum's side door with names and addresses of Duluthians who had requested Soviet pen friends. The man slipped out of the museum, handed me the poster rolled up in newspaper, and disappeared back inside.

The train trip to Petrozavodsk took twelve hours. We had sleeper compartments, but hardly anyone slept. A few tried, but the rest of us were too noisy. Someone had brought beer. Someone else had brought slivovitz, a strong plum brandy purchased during our seven hours in Yugo-slavia. Someone else had brought Jack Daniel's, wrapped in shirts and tucked in the bottom of a suitcase all the way from Minnesota. Despite the frowns of the babushka who tended the samovar at the end of the car, we left the doors to the compartments open and wandered up and down the narrow hallway, pouring drinks and laughing. The night pressed black against the windows as the train chugged north through bog land and forests, and I pushed the window down to feel the cool wind against my face and breathe in the piney fragrance. The babushka yelled at me, and I pushed the window up again. Tom was quiet; for him, perhaps more than for anyone else, the trip was about to change. Instead of exploring the city on his own, chatting with locals and going where he pleased, he knew that in Petrozavodsk he would have to become part of the group, under the control of Intourist. This quieted his cheerful nature, and he lay back on his bunk while all around him the rest of the group laughed and drank beer out of smuggled-in cans. In Petrozavodsk the trip would change for me too, but I was looking forward to it; my reporting would have to get sharper and more focused because I would have to file a story every evening for the next day's paper.

Looming over all of us—but over Brooks, especially—was the fact that we still had no idea how we would be received. Our itinerary called for four days in Petrozavodsk, but the details were still unknown. Would the mayor see us? Would the visit be nothing more than Intourist bus trips? Would the sister-city proposal be addressed—or be rejected? Shortly before leaving Duluth, Brooks had heard that the Soviets were opposed to the Duluth-Petrozavodsk matchup, but he had kept this information quiet and forged ahead. All of us were curious about what the next four days would hold. I think that uncertainty fueled the gaiety and celebration of the train ride: we knew the trip was about to become more serious.

I spent the early evening hours playing hangman with Tom Gildersleeve as the train rattled north through the forests of Karelia. Tom was a tall, cheerful sixteen-year-old who had come on this trip to practice his Russian, which he was studying at Duluth East High School. In Moscow, he kept disappearing into strange Ladas that drove off into the night, reappearing some time later with another fur hat; by now, he had acquired four of them and was down an equal number of pairs of jeans. He had brought along a Polaroid camera, and he planned to make friends in Petrozavodsk by what Brooks called "Polaroid diplomacy"—asking strangers if he could take their picture, and then letting them watch the image develop right before their eyes.

Late in the evening, word began trickling back that a man from Petrozavodsk was on the train. Eventually the man himself appeared, slender and serious, with neatly combed dark hair, dressed in a suit and tie, even though it was the middle of the night. His name was Oleg Ozhorovskii, and he was the deputy chairman of the Petrozavodsk city council. Could it be pure coincidence that put him on the same train with the happy delegation from Duluth? He and Brooks sat down to talk in one of the compartments. Neill Atkins and Richard Braun, two Duluth city councilors, crammed in as well. Tom Morgan and Masha were summoned to translate. I hung around the doorway, doing my best to listen. Ozhorovskii's news was good. He told Brooks that Petrozavodsk had great plans for our visit—tours of a paper mill, a school, the Palace of Young Pioneers, and museums. Visits to the homes of ordinary citizens. Even better news was this: a meeting with the mayor. "The schedule is tight because we would like you to see as much of our city as possible," he said.

I am not sure if the other people in that train car realized what momentous news this was. Brooks's demeanor was as calm and low-key as usual, but inside, I know, he was filled with tremendous relief. Until that moment, he had not known if his big plan, if this grand gesture of *just showing up* was going to pay off; until that moment, he had not known if the mayor would receive us. I'm not sure if anyone else realized how much Brooks had put himself on the line. Neill Atkins pulled out the Jack Daniel's. "A toast!" he said, but Oleg shook his head. Gorbachev had instituted a program to curb excessive drinking—for generations a serious problem in Russia—and he was taking it seriously. A few people held out their glasses anyway, and as we toasted, Oleg slipped away.

Outside the window, the sun began to rise. The forests looked like the forests of northern Minnesota, aspen and birch just beginning to turn gold. A light drizzle streaked the windows, and the rain came down harder as we pulled into Petrozavodsk station. I pushed the window down again and stuck my head out, trying to get a glimpse of the city, but all I could see was the platform, crowded with the usual old people you see hanging around train stations, waiting for loved ones to disembark. They stood under colorful umbrellas, many of them holding bunches of gladiolas.

We shuddered to a stop, and I hauled my duffle bag down from the shelf and stepped outside. The old people surged toward me, toward all of us. They thrust flowers in our direction. The thirty-three of us stood bewildered in the gentle morning rain as the kindly wrinkled faces pressed close. They chattered with excitement, all at once, interrupting each other, and it took me a few startled seconds to realize that they were chattering in English. "Hello, Duluth!" they said. "Are the hills still green? Does the Aerial Bridge still go up and down?" They handed flowers to each of the astonished Duluthians. I stared at them and tried to figure out who they were, why they were speaking English, why they might think the Aerial Bridge no longer worked, how they knew there even was an Aerial Bridge. I had completely forgotten Erkki Leppo and his tales of American Finns in the USSR. I touched one of the old people on the arm, to get her attention. "How do you know the Aerial Bridge?" I asked.

The woman smiled at me. "I was born in Cloquet," she said.

·

Enter Mayme

....

WE FILED INTO THE MAYOR'S RECEPTION ROOM, A LIT-
tle cowed by the solemnity of the occasion. We had been
in Petrozavodsk only a day or so, and after our casual and
anonymous freewheeling through Moscow and Leningrad,
the tightly packed schedule and welcoming throngs in
Petrozavodsk were overwhelming. Gaggles of uniformed
schoolchildren pressed lapel pins, flowers, and paper doves
into our hands; we were herded onto buses and hauled off
to tour day care centers and schools, as well as places farther afield—mills and factories, where we traipsed through
polishing rooms cloudy with marble dust, and machine
sheds stacked high with tractor parts. We were well chaper-
oned, with not just one Intourist guide but two. Masha had
come with us from Leningrad, and Petrozavodsk provided a
guide as well, a stocky red-haired woman named Ludmilla
Schmidt who wore knee-high leather boots. Everywhere we
went, people welcomed us with wide smiles and trinkets
and food—oh, so much food! "Please to have a leetle snock,"
they would say in their charming accented English, and the
little snack would turn out to be a lavish spread of meat and
cheese and tomatoes and cake and bread and tea and sometimes vodka. Joey and I began to dread the snacks, since the

hotel fed us well at breakfast and dinner. But the offerings were sociable and welcoming; to turn them down would be rude. We were eating heavily, at every stop, all day long.

Earlier that day, we had visited the Yuri Andropov Palace of Young Pioneers, where children in Karelian folk dress played the zither, tumbled through a gymnastics routine, sang, and danced. Three girls in embroidered dresses and striped socks stepped forward in unison, holding out a loaf of bread with a dish of salt embedded in the center. They presented it to the youngest member of our group, Shanda Braun, a thin, blonde thirteen-year-old girl who was traveling with her parents (and subsisting on the cans of tuna fish and jars of peanut butter that her mother had smuggled into the country in her suitcase; Shanda was not a fan of Russian food). She accepted the ceremonial loaf of bread and then looked around nervously. "What do I do with it now?" she whispered. "What am I supposed to do with it?"

In preparation for this trip, the Duluth group had memorized a few Russian phrases (thank you, please, excuse me) and had learned the old Russian folk song "Ochi Chyornye" ("Dark Eyes"), just in case we should ever be called on to perform, but we had not learned about the bread and salt, which is a traditional welcome in western Russia. We watched Shanda in silence as she stood in the middle of the room, the loaf of bread balanced on a red and white embroidered cloth that was draped over her upturned palms. Masha came to her rescue. "It is tradition to pinch off the bread and dip it in the salt," she said. "But since you probably want to keep it, you don't have to do that." Shanda's tense shoulders relaxed, and someone kindly took the bread away.

And now all thirty-three of us were in the mayor's reception room, a large, airy space with one wall built of Karelian stone, and another all of windows streaming with sunlight. Mayor Vladimir Dorchakov stood at a podium on a low stage. City officials and dignitaries sat in a row at his side, and Brooks was invited to join them. The rest of us found seats at the many small tables; at each place sat a heavy green goblet and a bottle of mineral water. Mayor Dorchakov looked like the quintessential Russian—stocky with wavy black hair and ruddy cheeks. "I am glad to meet you," he began in Russian, and Masha stood up and began translating. "I want to tell you about our city, how we live, what we are doing, and what problems we have."

And he did. He told us and told us and told us, and the sunlight warmed my face, and my eyes drooped, and the room grew warm, and the Russian voice droned on and on, an unintelligible but not unpleasant and somewhat soothing ...

I jerked my head up, looked around. All around the room, Minnesota heads were bobbing. None of us had gotten any sleep on the train, we had spent the day touring the city and being honored everywhere we went, and by now we were running on fumes, adrenaline, and those frequent, heavy snacks. This was the first chance we had had to sit down. My eyes fluttered again, and I opened a bottle of water and filled my glass. Drinking would give me something to do; it would keep me awake. As I sipped, Dorchakov talked and Masha translated. He talked about the history of Petrozavodsk. He talked about World War II. He described the city's buildings and sports facilities and parks. He talked about the need for world peace. I sneaked a glance at my watch. A half hour had gone by. Then forty minutes. An hour, and still he spoke, honoring us, as Russians do, by the length of his speech. Meanwhile, my bottle of water had done what bottles of water will do, and I began furtively glancing around for a bathroom. At the back of the room I saw double doors that led out into the hall, and I stared at them with longing. I didn't dare get up, though; I didn't know my way around the building, I didn't want to disrupt the speech—surely he was almost done—I didn't know how to ask for directions, and I didn't know the Russian words for WOMEN or MEN and feared heading through the wrong door. I was trapped, and I was not the only one. At tables all around me, I saw that nervous wide-eyed look that meant others were in the same state. On stage, Masha began to falter. She stumbled over phrases, shook her head, started over. A blonde woman seated beside her stood up. "She is exhausted," the blonde woman announced crisply, and Masha sat down. Dorchakov did not miss a beat; he continued to talk, and the blonde woman picked up the translation with great energy. Her name, I found out later, was Mayme Sevander. She had a prominent nose, impressive penciled eyebrows, and a sturdy build, and even from across the room, even in my bleary state, I could tell she was a woman of power.

Dorchakov ran out of topics and began to read aloud from the newspaper. Mayme continued to translate unflaggingly. She could have translated all day and all night, I thought, and still have been fresh and strong in the morning. An hour and a quarter passed. An hour and a half. I opened another bottle of mineral water. It was a fight between my drooping eyes and my full bladder. I drank and tried not to fear the consequences. My ears perked up, though, when the mayor finally began to talk about the sister-city relationship. "We are very glad to see you. We welcome you here," he said. "We want to tell you what we are thinking about, and we are thinking about peace. We would like to visit Duluth someday. If good relations are maintained between our two countries, there's no doubt we would be there someday. And if we visit, we will bring actors, painters, and musicians." I wrote down his words in my notebook. This was tantamount to a promise that the sister-city relationship would be approved. The trip was officially a success. Brooks must be very relieved.

That evening, after dinner, we were herded back onto the bus and driven to the Finnish Theater to meet with the intelligentsia—actors and professors and poets and musicians. I was worried; I was expected to file a story for the *Duluth News-Tribune*, and I needed to write it and call the newsroom before I went to bed. Moscow was nine hours ahead of Minnesota, so I knew I had plenty of time to make deadline, but I worried about making the phone call itself. Calling the United States was more complicated than I had realized; I couldn't just pick up the phone and dial but needed a Russian-speaking person to help me reserve the call with the hotel operator, who then had to place the call through Moscow. I was told that it sometimes took hours for a connection to go through.

At the Finnish Theater we were served another lavish spread of food, and then the other delegation members filed into an adjacent room to listen to a concert. I stayed at the table, lingering over coffee and talking with Sasha Trubin, a journalist with *Komsomolets*. We tried to explain our very different newspapers to each other. His paper, which came out three times a week, carried no advertising. The reporters did not write about crimes or accidents or other bad news; other than feature stories, it was not clear to me what they did write about. He asked me repeatedly how big my paper was. In circulation? I asked. Or in size? But neither question made sense to him because neither was the way they did business. Soviet papers did not depend on readers buying them or on advertisers taking out ads; their revenue came from the state. The papers were a standard size, the same every day, and were often posted up on notice boards for people to read. "Our paper tries to have 60 percent ads, and 40 percent news," I said.

"But how big is it?" he asked again. "How many pages?"

"It depends on how many ads there are. It changes each day," I said. And Sasha shook his head. This did not make sense to him.

We decided we needed to talk about all of this further. According to the official itinerary, the Duluthians were scheduled to spend the next evening visiting the homes of ordinary citizens. I figured this would be a good opportunity for me to peel off and see something a little less scripted, so Sasha and I made plans. I would get Joey, and Sasha would grab his photographer friend, Oleg, and the four of us would go somewhere and talk about journalism. We agreed to meet the next evening in the lobby of the Hotel Sevarnaya.

Back in my hotel room, I enlisted the help of Mike Jaros to place a phone call to the newsroom. Mike was a state legislator from Duluth; he spoke passable Russian, and it was he who had arranged our Yugo Air flight from Belgrade.

He was the younger brother of Karl, the photographer who had smuggled money into America inside of his accordion. While I started scribbling the guts of a story in my notebook, Mike called the hotel operator. After a bit of back-and-forth, he hung up. "She says she will call you when the call goes through," he said. He looked a little uncertain. "It might be a long time."

I finished writing my story—a quick take on the lengthy meeting with the mayor, and his promising words at the end—and then I sat and waited. Everyone else had gone off to the hotel bar for a nightcap, but I had to file my story. I picked up *Anna Karenina* and read a few pages, nodded off, woke up, walked around the room to stay awake, but the phone did not ring. The hour grew late; Joey came back and climbed into bed. I sat up, my back propped with pillows, my bedside lamp on, and stared at the phone, which did not ring. Long after midnight, I finally turned off the light, my notes and story at the ready on the table next to the phone. My editor would be worried about me; the night desk was saving a hole for my story. A telegram? Should I try to send a telegram? Wouldn't that be excessive? Was it even possible? Maybe the call would go through yet. I slept fitfully, waking frequently, listening for the phone, which never rang.

The next day was a blur of touring—was that the day we took the bus to the Onega Tractor Plant? Or to Kondopoga, to see the marble works? Or maybe it was the day we took the hydrofoil across Lake Onega to the island of Kizhi, to walk among the elaborate domed wooden churches that had been built without a single nail. Whatever we did, we were certainly shepherded on and off the bus, fed meal

after meal, and presented with souvenir lapel pins. We were
expected to hand out little American-Soviet crossed-flag
pins in return. This exchange of lapel pins troubled me; I
was a journalist, after all, accompanying the delegation
but not a member of the delegation. While I had nothing
against making friends, that wasn't why I was along. I was
there as an objective observer, there to bear witness, not
to take part in what Brooks called "citizen diplomacy," but
I had no way of making the Russians understand this. To
them, I was just one of the Americans—granted, one who
stood off to the side writing in a notebook, but one of the
Americans nonetheless. They expected me to abide by their
schedule, attend their events, take part in their activities,
and accept their gifts. Gifts! Journalists can't accept gifts!
The trip became, for me, an internal battle between journal-
istic ethics and humanity; to refuse would have been inex-
plicable to them and crushingly rude. To accept would be
to appear biased and open to bribes. I was never quite sure
how to play it.

One afternoon at one of the schools, a small Russian
girl noticed me sitting on the sidelines while everyone else
was dancing. She peeked at me a few times and then ran up,
tugged my hand, and led me out to the floor. What could
I do? How could I explain to this tiny beribboned brown-
eyed girl that I was not supposed to take part in such things
as dancing with the Russians? Saying that I just wanted to
watch—even if I had been able to say it in a language she
understood—would sound creepy. So we danced, and when
the dance was over, I reached into my pocket and pulled out
a crossed-flag lapel pin, which I had been hoarding for just
such an emergency.

The girl darted off across the gymnasium floor, and I lost her in the crowd. But minutes later, as we were filing out of the room, I felt a tug on my sleeve and turned to see her at my side. She beamed up at me with a huge bright smile and poured a double-fistful of lapel pins into my cupped hands.

That evening we gathered in the hotel lobby to board the bus for the visits to homes of ordinary citizens. Thirty-one Duluthians bobbed around, trying to find their host families, while off to the side Joey and I craned our necks, looking for Sasha and Oleg. When I spotted them, we waved and started over, weaving through the crowd, but a brisk and familiar voice stopped me. "Sooo, what have we here?" I looked up to see the formidable blonde translator from the mayor's office. Sasha and Oleg looked at us uneasily. "What are you doing here?" she asked the men. "Joey and I are going to go with them this evening," I said, to which Mayme Sevander said, "Oh, no, you are not." She turned and spoke sharply to them in Russian, and they nodded and backed up and apologized and said a hasty goodbye to Joey and me and disappeared.

"You have been invited to people's homes!" Mayme scolded. "They have gone to great trouble to invite you, to prepare for you. They have made food for you and invited guests to meet you. They are expecting you! It would be very rude of you not to go." Joey and I looked at each other. Here it was again, the endless conundrum of the trip. I should not have to be tied to the ceremonial meetings of the group—I should be free to break away and report where I saw stories, as I had in Moscow. I tried to explain this to Mayme, but she wasn't listening. She was consulting the itinerary to see which home Joey and I had been assigned, and then she crumpled it up and shoved it into her pocket. She put one arm around my shoulder and one arm around Joey's shoulder, and she said, "You will come with me to my house." Her embrace was friendly enough, but it was strong; it meant that I was being almost frog marched out of the hotel and up the street. As we stepped along in Mayme's grip, I caught a glimpse of Sasha and Oleg, standing off in the shadows near our hotel. They watched us frog-march away.

In Mayme's apartment, the television was on with the sound turned down. She stooped to fiddle with the knobs, and I wondered if this was to draw attention to the fact that she owned a color TV—a rare privilege in the Soviet Union in 1986. It flickered quietly in the corner all evening. Her guests were waiting in the living room: her blonde daughter, Stella; Stella's dark-haired husband, Igor Ryzhenkov, in a crew-necked sweater; Mayme's brother, Paul Corgan, a stocky man with thinning gray hair; an older, dark-haired man named Saul Wagner; and a small, sweet-faced woman named Ruth Niskanen. Mayme's young blond grandson, Andy, ran in and out. Mayme made introductions—Brooks was with us, and Joyce Benson, a Duluth city councilor, and Barb Hakala, a Duluth teacher—and then she urged us to relax, have some vodka, enjoy a bite to eat.

More food! Joey and I looked at each other. Mayme's long wooden dining room table was loaded with delicacies. Open-faced caviar sandwiches, smoked cod and tomato sandwiches, coffee, vodka (with cranberry syrup for the women), a silver samovar of tea. As the evening wore on, Stella disappeared into the kitchen from time to time, returning with more desserts: a box of chocolates, some

....

Russian marshmallows—sweeter than American marshmallows and crunchy—and a heavy cake topped with whipped
cream.

Saul and Ruth both spoke excellent, fluent English. This
should not have been a surprise; they, like Mayme and her
brother, were American by birth. They had been among the
crowd that had greeted us that first morning at the train station. Everyone that rainy morning, they told us, was American born and had come as children to the Soviet Union in
the 1920s and 1930s. I listened, more amazed than I should
have been. It was Erkki Leppo's concerns come to life, sitting in front of me on a sofa in a fifth-floor apartment somewhere in the north of Russia on a chilly September evening,
drinking tea. My head swam; it was almost too much to com-
prehend. They were American born? Didn't that make them
American citizens? Or did it? If their parents had become
Soviet citizens, had their children's citizenship automatically followed?

As the evening wore on, they told their stories, but
only abbreviated, cheerful versions. Saul was from New
York. Ruth was from Palo, on Minnesota's Iron Range. And
Mayme and Paul were from Superior, Wisconsin. All had
been small children when Lenin put out the call of "Workers of the world, unite!" and their parents had listened
and obeyed. "Have you ever been back?" I asked, and Saul
looked at me with his sad, dark eyes and finally said, "It's
complicated." Ruth was twelve years old when she left the
Iron Range for Petrozavodsk in 1932 with her mother, her
stepfather, and her two brothers. She still had dreams about
that sturdy house in Palo that her father had built, but she
had never seen it again.

Mayme and Paul's story was the most dramatic; it was

their father who had urged the other Finns to go. Oscar
Corgan had spent much of the 1930s traveling throughout the upper Midwest, speaking at Finn Halls, spreading
the word of Communism, and persuading Finnish families
to emigrate. He moved his wife and children—Mayme and
Paul and their little sister, Aino to Petrozavodsk in 1936,
and Oscar was arrested and executed in the purges the next
year. Mayme glossed over this point fairly quickly, and Ruth
and Saul did not tell us the sad particulars of their lives—we
were a sister-city delegation, after all, there to make friends,
not to uncover the troubling tragedies of their country's
past. "We have our problems, there is no doubt—as they do
in all countries," Mayme said in her brisk and no-nonsense
way, and the others listened. "We lost our own father in the
purges. We're not going to deny that those things happen.
A person cannot remain bitter until the end of his life. It was
tough, but we are fighters. We expected it to be tough. We
are trained to be fighters." The American Finns, she said,
built Petrozavodsk. The Finnish Theater, where we had met
with the intelligentsia, had been built by American Finns,
who brought tools and lumber and cash and supplies with
them from the United States. The sidewalks, the plumbing, many of the buildings, the cross-country ski factory,
the lumber mill in nearby Matroosa—all had been built by
American Finns. Mayme told us this with great pride, at the
same time taking great care to refute many of the negative
things that Erkki Leppo had told me. How did she know of
Leppo? How had she seen the story that I had written for the
Duluth paper? She brushed my questions away with great
impatience. "It is not important," she said. "I see everything."

This, I figured, was almost certainly true.

Stella had disappeared into the kitchen while Mayme was talking, and now she emerged with one last dessert—blueberry pie. I had eaten the cod sandwiches, I had sampled the caviar, I had accepted chocolates and cake and marshmallows and had tossed back a shot of vodka, which left me slightly dizzy. The pie bobbed closer . . . Saul bent down and whispered in my ear. "Just try a little," he advised kindly. "She'll feel bad if you don't."

Every night I went back to my hotel room while everyone else was merrily winding down at the bar, and I wrote a story for the *News-Tribune* about the day's events. Every night I asked one of the Russian-speaking members of the delegation to help me place the call. And every night I waited, in vain, for the call to go through. Not once did I reach the newsroom; each night the hotel operator instructed me to wait, and each night I fell asleep with my notebook and pen by the bed, my story not yet dictated. I hoped they weren't worried about us back in Duluth, but Duluth seemed so distant, it was hard to be concerned.

On our last night in Petrozavodsk, the mayor threw a farewell banquet for us at the Kavkaz Restaurant. We filled the room; Neill Atkins and Brooks sat at the head table with the mayor and matched him toast for toast. (Dorchakov, cognizant of Gorbachev's restrictions on alcohol, toasted with wine instead of the more traditional vodka, a decision that might have—who knows?—saved the lives of several delegation members.) During his farewell speech, which did not last as long as his welcome speech, he confirmed the sister-city friendship and promised to send a delegation to Duluth in the spring to sign the official documents. Even more exciting was his promise to send three runners in June to take part in Grandma's Marathon—what he called Marathon Babushki. Russian runners in Duluth's race along the North Shore! This certainly was not anything like declaring our city a nuclear-free zone; it was clear that now that the Russians had agreed to this friendship, the story was just beginning. Duluth was going to have to work hard to keep up its end of the deal.

We left Petrozavodsk by train that night and arrived in Moscow in the morning. Our flight would leave early the next day, and I knew I needed to make one more attempt to file a story. That evening, Tom Morgan negotiated with the receptionist at the front desk, and this time it worked. Shortly after eight o'clock, when the other members of the delegation were out seeing the town, the phone rang in my hotel room. Keith Thomsen, working the weekend shift in Duluth, was on the other end. "Can you take dictation?" I asked.

"Hertzbach?" he said. "Are you in Russia?"

I knew the connection was shaky, and I knew to talk fast. I kept the story short. Dateline, Moscow. "The mayor of the northern Soviet town of Petrozavodsk has all but promised a Duluth delegation that the two towns will become official sister cities soon . . ."

When I was done, Keith said, "So why didn't you call? Everyone's been wondering where you are." And it sounded so normal, so reasonable, him on one end of the phone in Duluth, me on the other end in Russia, just the way we had planned, that I wasn't sure how to answer. Just saying that the calls hadn't gone through sounded lame; foreign correspondents file stories from all over the world every day. But it was the only excuse I had. Keith told me that readers had been calling the paper, asking where I was and why the paper wasn't running the promised daily reports, and finally Larry Fortner had run a story explaining that communication had been faulty and that the reports would have to wait until my return. Nothing makes a reporter feel less worthy than not making deadline, and here I had blown deadline four days in a row on what was almost certainly the biggest story of my life.

We left the country the same way we had arrived, in the wee hours of the morning, stumbling with exhaustion, slightly confused. There had been much drinking and celebrating, a sense of melancholy on the last night of this strange and exotic trip, and we had all stayed up late toasting with (I am sorry to tell Mr. Gorbachev this) vodka. We were told to gather in the hotel lobby, packed and ready to go, by four o'clock in the morning. This is just about the most impossible hour there could be. Three o'clock, well, you could just stay up. Five isn't that bad. But getting up and getting packed at four was tough. Groggily, Joey and I stuffed our clothes into our duffle bags and bump-bump-bumped them down the stairs and huddled in the chilly, dim lobby. I had almost no gifts for folks back home; I had never seen the inside of a berioska shop and surely was the only one of the thirty-three who had no stacking dolls, no flowered scarves, no lacquered boxes, no painted spoons. All I had were the abacus and the little metal cars I had bought at Detsky Mir on our first day in Moscow, the poster from the atheism museum, and a double-fistful of lapel pins from the little brown-eyed girl.

One by one, the delegation members yawned their way into the lobby. The Intourist bus would be here at any minute to take us to the airport for the very long journey home. Over at the front desk, the clerks were whispering in great agitation, and then I heard one of them call my name. I drifted over, and they scolded and twittered, and I listened in confusion and finally grew to understand their concern: my phone call. That fifteen-minute call to the newsroom; I could not leave the country until I paid for it. "Can't I just give you my credit card?" I asked foolishly, but no, an American credit card was of no use in a Soviet hotel in 1986. "You must pay cash," they said. The problem was, they didn't know how much the phone call cost. These kinds of charges normally take days to determine, they said, and if they had known I was leaving the next morning, they would never have allowed me to place the call in the first place. Tom Morgan stepped over and tried to negotiate for me, but the receptionists were upset. "We should not have allowed it," they kept saying. They clicked their abacus beads back and forth and muttered to each other, and one of them disappeared into the back room for a long while. The bus was going to be here at any moment, my flight was due to take off in three hours, and I was in danger of being left behind because I had made a phone call? I was not frightened, but I was nervous. I really did not want to stay here any longer; I was quite ready to go home. It's one thing to blow deadline; it's another thing to miss the flight home.

Finally the clerk emerged from the back room. "One hundred and fifty dollars," she said. "That phone call will be one hundred and fifty dollars. Cash only, American dollars." Other people in the delegation had reached into their pockets for rubles to help me. But American dollars only? Who had any, or that much? Hands emerged from pockets, empty. I unzipped my little purse with trembling fingers. How much money had I exchanged when I first got here? How much was left? I couldn't remember. I pulled out my hoard of greenbacks and counted out the tens and twenties: Exactly one hundred and fifty dollars. It was as if they had somehow known. Good thing I had skipped those berioska shops; good thing I hadn't squandered any money on stacking dolls. I had just enough money to get out of the country. I handed the bills over to the still fussing clerks, grabbed my duffle bag, and headed out the door. As I climbed onto the bus, Brooks gave me a smile. "Welcome aboard," he said. "Let's go home."

Back in Duluth, writing the stories of that trip was difficult. Jet lag engulfed me, and every day I struggled out of bed after a sleepless night, drove to the office, and wrote two stories for the next day's paper—one story about life in Russia, and one story about the experiences of the Duluthians. Then I crawled home and collapsed until midnight, when I slammed awake. I lay unsleeping in the dark, night after night, thinking over all I had seen and all I had done and all the stories that I needed to write and all the stories that I wanted to write. I knew that what I was producing for the newspaper wasn't exactly what I wanted to say. The Russian trip was bigger and more complicated than a series of twenty-inch newspaper pieces could reflect; it was richer than I could portray dashing off two hasty stories a day. The ball cap–wearing street sweepers with their straw brooms; Alexander, the survivor of the siege of Leningrad; the museum worker slipping out the side door with my poster, eager for an American correspondent; Mayme and her formidable eyebrows; the fierce babushkas who were stationed everywhere; Sasha and Oleg, the curious journalists—they all jostled together in my brain, past the wooden churches of Kizhi, the cafeterias of Leningrad, the broad boulevards of Petrozavodsk sweeping down to the shore of Lake Onega, so much like our Lake Superior.

I was grateful to Fortner for sending me to Russia, certainly the best story of my career. But Russia had turned out to be much more than that, and in many ways it had transcended my job as a journalist. It had caused me to reshape my interests and rethink my place in the world.

·

A Month in the South

....

IN THE WEEKS AND MONTHS AFTER MY RETURN FROM
Russia, the newsroom became a festival of change, with
reporters switching beats, or quitting, and new people walking in the door, overflowing with enthusiasm and wit. This
was the tail end of the robust years; throughout most of
the 1980s, we had published big fat newspapers each day,
with tons of advertising, and with penetration—that unfortunate term used to describe how many home subscribers
we had—over 90 percent, one of the highest in the country.
Everybody read us. They might not have liked us or agreed
with us, but they couldn't do without us. That was even one
of our mouthy slogans: *Love us or hate us, but read us.* We
had no true competitors—just television, which we sneered
at (even while madly scribbling down notes on stories that
we had missed), and small community papers, which we pil-
laged for ideas, and, every now and then, for staff: the *Superior Evening Telegram* across the St. Louis Bay, and the little
weeklies up the Shore and dotting the Range. "It's not news
until we say it's news," we said with a bit of a swagger, and
we were only half kidding.

The newsroom had expanded, with a new addition four
steps up, right over the press room. The original newsroom

with the battered desks and linoleum floor was remodeled into spacious digs for features, sports, and the copy desk; the new space, with neat rows of beige cubicles and sober gray carpeting, was given over to news. Fortner moved into a big windowed office that looked out on the steep avenue and Lake Superior, but he always said it never felt quite right; he liked the cramped old office that faced the government buildings of the Civic Center. It seemed more appropriate, he said, given the newspaper's watchdog role. We moved into our cubicles before construction was quite done, and working in the din was a challenge; it was hard to conduct phone interviews amid the jarring cacophony of jackhammers and power drills and the shrieking whine of circular saws. I held the phone tight to one ear, plugged the other ear, tried to find a third hand with which to take notes. Every now and then, the lights flickered, and we all leaped to store whatever we had on our screens. I wasn't sure I was going to like the new addition; I loved that crammed old newsroom, saw character and history where others saw dirt and inconvenience. Yes, with a cubicle I had a bigger desk, and more privacy, and carpeted walls where I could pin up postcards and phone numbers and pictures of my dog. But it made the place seem unnervingly orderly and professional. Like a bank. Like a career.

The lovely, deadline-challenged Diane quit and moved to Texas. Fortner left and was replaced by a new editor, Bob Jodon, "the man with three first names." The *Star Tribune* raided our ranks; they had already taken Chris Ison; now they took Doug Smith and Dennis Buster and Larry Oakes and M. L. Levandowski, all of whom packed up and headed for the tall buildings and busy freeways of the Twin Cities.

Everyone, it seemed, eventually moved to the Twin Cities, or wanted to. Everyone but me. I was still the biggest Duluth booster you ever saw, dragging people on hikes along Congdon Creek or up Seven Bridges Road, or driving up the Shore for French-pressed coffee and Sunday brunch at the Scenic Café. (Which many of my friends said they loved because it was just like a restaurant in the Cities. They had no idea how that annoyed me. Or maybe they did.)

We plugged the holes in the staff with new hires: A tall, loud redheaded guy named John Myers came from a small daily in Wisconsin. He tacked up pictures of fish he had caught and deer he had killed, and in December he entwined his cubicle with silver tinsel and musical Christmas lights. After a few days the managers made him turn the sound off, because the constant tinny carols annoyed the cops reporter, but since the colored lights flashed in time with the music, you could always tell what song was playing just by looking. Some of us sang along quietly under our breath.

A tall blond guy named Doug Iverson, who had been editor of the *Minnesota Daily*, showed up fresh off an internship in Pittsburgh, where he had lived for a summer in a sweltering attic apartment. He moved into a slightly less sweltering apartment in Duluth's Central Hillside, which he dubbed the "Hillside Hilton," and he and Myers quickly became bookends at most *News-Tribune* after-hours events, two guys, each six feet four, one quiet, one loud, both hilarious. We hired a guy named Chris Thompson to cover Superior; a hard-as-nails reporter named Julie Bell, to cover city hall; a copy editor from *USA Today*, Erik Ninomiya, who quickly became my best friend; a short, motormouthed photographer named Steve Stearns, who trudged around dripping with scanners and cameras and police radios. He had worked at the paper in Worthington, in southern Minnesota, and was used to driving long distances for a story and eating in the car; the reporters there had nicknamed him "Meals on Wheels." He nicknamed me "MegaHertz."

I couldn't help but notice that all of the new hires were younger than I was. I was no longer the whiz kid with the braids pinned on top of my head; I had long since unfurled my hair and, at thirty, was getting to be a senior person in the room. The new whiz kids all had degrees, and some had advanced degrees. Fellow reporter Susan Stanich and I were the only ones who hadn't finished college, and she was so well read, such a great writer and dogged reporter, that in her case the lack of degree seemed immaterial. But me, I worried. Somewhere along the way, working for the paper had gone from being something I was doing until I figured out what I really wanted to do, to being something I was, well, *doing*. My life's work, apparently. Was this what I wanted? What about those broader stories I wanted to tell? What about fiction? What about living in a Nova Scotia cabin with a bunch of cats? Even though I loved reporting— after ten years the newsroom still had that creative and freewheeling atmosphere that reminded me of my days on the high school yearbook—I felt like I had never really made a decision about a career. I had just fallen into journalism one day, and as various doors opened—the opportunity to copyedit, to report, to travel to Russia—I had pushed on through. But none of this had been a deliberate choice, and it now seemed time to start directing myself instead of just amiably agreeing to whatever came my way. The trip to Russia was starting to fade in my mind, but not its revelation: that daily deadline journalism wasn't all I wanted.

At home, I began writing fiction again. I took a fiction-writing class from Joe Maiolo at the University of Minnesota Duluth (where another student pronounced one of my stories "as boring as a bowl of unsalted oatmeal"); I swapped short stories with Katy Read, and we critiqued each other's work. When I walked Toby in the mornings along the cowslip-choked creek that cut through the woods behind my house, I spun the stories out in my head; I could picture the scenes, hear the dialogue, and it all seemed quite brilliant until I got home and wrestled it down onto paper. I saw symbolism everywhere. Selling my Chevy Monza was no longer an ordinary act of selling a car; it was symbolic of moving on, and I started a short story called "Wheels," which I labored over, working it and reworking it. I went duck hunting with a boyfriend and his father, and—crouched in the duck boat, hidden in the cattails—I looked up at the pink sky of early morning and wondered what it would be like to have grown up with killing as part of my family tradition. I went down to Canal Park on summer evenings and watched the glittering salties pass under the Aerial Bridge and imagined someone gliding out of my life the way the boats glided out of the harbor. Everywhere I looked, the world was laden with meaning, and I felt overflowing with stories I wanted to tell.

At home, I taped sheets of paper to the wall by my desk, one page for each story, to keep track of where I had sent them. The lists began with big magazines that paid, but quickly worked their way to journals that only sent contributor copies—journals that I seldom read but had seen listed

in *Writer's Market.* I was rejected so many times that sometimes I had to tape up additional sheets. As each story came
back in the mail, I put it in a fresh envelope and mailed it
out again the same day. When a story began to look ragged,
I typed a fresh copy, editing and rewriting as I worked.

At work, the newsroom began feeling the pinch of the
sinking economy. Circulation dropped for the first time
that I could remember. Classified ads, which had always
been an enormous moneymaker, began to drop off too.
Jodon was told to trim space, and our big fat news hole
shrank by an alarming 10 percent. When a reporter or editor quit, we shuffled the staff around instead of hiring a
replacement. For those of us who were restless—that would
be me—it was a great opportunity because there were now
more open positions than staffers to fill them. I was wooed
from many corners—did I want to go back to the night copy
desk, this time as a supervisor? Was I interested in covering
the county board, now that they were going through a crucial budget process that was sure to yield a string of Page
One stories? Or how about the education beat—that might
be coming open soon, was I interested? I had my pick of
jobs, and I tried out several, looking for a good fit. None felt
exactly right. I poured out my career angst in long letters to
Pam Miller, up in Alaska. Six-, eight-, ten-page letters filled
with newsroom machinations and ambitions.

"I like the idea of being News Editor on the night desk,
and having my days free for hikes, reading, UMD classes,"
I wrote. "But then I decided that wasn't the position I could
learn the most from, and I turned it down." I settled for a
while on a day general assignment job—the mix of assignments, something new every day, appealed to me. The sen-

sible and tough Georgia Swing was promoted to executive city editor, and I reported to her. She had a million ideas, some good, some not so good, and my job was to take them and turn a story a day for the front page. This proved to be fun but nerve-wracking. Accuracy was always crucial, but when a story was headed for the front page, the stakes went up. I remember that year of working for Georgia as a blur of adrenaline and dread, stress and excitement. Knowing that my story was going on the front page made me nervous. I printed out my stories, yellow-highlighted every fact, and double checked, and triple checked. When a mistake crept through, I was so upset my whole body grew cold. The chill started in my hands—maybe they felt to blame for typing the inaccuracy in the first place—and ran up my arms straight to my heart. I called someone a psychiatrist when he was a psychologist. I gave someone the wrong middle name. A copy editor ruined my feature on bed and breakfasts by calling them, in a sixty-point headline, "Bread and breakfasts." With each error we had to write a groveling memo, explaining how we had made the mistake and how we would keep from making mistakes in the future. It was humiliating, and I resented it; we all resented it. We typed our memos while gritting our teeth. Reporters hate a lot of things—not being called back, getting scooped, being on vacation when the big story breaks. But we hate mistakes more than anything else.

We talked about this after work, over beers at the Pickwick, sitting around the big wooden table under the dangling taxidermy fish—the stress of perfection. Some of my friends maintained that all newspaper stories have factual errors and there's nothing we can do about it; they are written and reported in such haste that there will always be things we don't know or don't understand, and so there will always be nuance or emphasis that is wrong. Even if no one calls to complain, they said, just assume you got something wrong anyway. I couldn't accept that point of view; it made me feel doomed.

Over time, delegations to and from Petrozavodsk became commonplace. There were so many you could no longer keep track—athletes and scientists and students and academics and musicians heading back and forth. At times it seemed like nearly everyone I knew was either just heading off to Russia or just coming back. Tom Morgan left the paper to teach Russian language at the College of St. Scholastica. He set up a language camp, sending Duluth students to Petrozavodsk to study Russian one summer, bringing Russian students to Duluth to study English the next. He also worked out an arrangement with a local book publisher, Pfeifer-Hamilton, to publish Mayme Sevander's memoirs, and she came to Duluth for an academic year to teach with Tom at St. Scholastica and write the book.

I thought Mayme was an interesting if formidable person, but I hoped she didn't do anything newsworthy while she was in town; I didn't want her to become my beat. But what did I want? I was restless in any beat I had. And then one day I came home to find a letter from *North Dakota Quarterly*. This was not a fat envelope containing my spurned story and a xeroxed rejection slip; this was a thin envelope with one sheet of paper inside, an actual letter. I dropped my coat onto a chair and ripped open the envelope while Toby pranced at my feet, eager to go out. The letter was from William Borden, the journal's fiction editor. He wanted to publish my short story "Ocean Boats" in their winter 1992 issue, more than a year away. "He wants to publish my story," I said, and then I said it again. (I often talked to my amiable and devoted dog, who listened well but never replied.) "Wow! *North Dakota Quarterly* wants to publish my story." Toby heard the excitement in my voice, and he grabbed a tennis ball and dashed to the door, his beautiful plumey tail wagging.

And then, just a week or two later, a second skinny envelope, this one from the editor of the *South Dakota Review*. They would publish "Watching the Sky," my duck-hunting story, in summer 1991. I solemnly ripped down the tracking sheets for those two stories and taped the acceptance letters onto the wall in their place. This news was thrilling, but it also produced a nagging grain of doubt. It's one thing to tell everyone that you're writing fiction; you can go on about it forever over beers or coffee, making it sound as great as you like. But once you're accepted for publication, anyone can read your work and judge for themselves whether you're any good. I had read those short stories over so many times I had lost all perspective; I had stopped revising them, because I had them so thoroughly memorized I could no longer imagine them any other way. And now they would be in print, for the entire vast readership of, well, of *North Dakota Quarterly* and *South Dakota Review* to read and judge. My little brother Tommy made sure my head didn't get too big. "Well, you've got the Dakotas covered," he said dryly. "Time to try a whole new part of the country."

At work, another door cracked open. A month-long fellowship at Duke University in North Carolina was up for

grabs. Knight-Ridder Newspapers offered these fellowships a few times a year to midcareer reporters, and usually it was the more experienced folks at the bigger papers
who won them—people from Philadelphia, Miami, San Jose.
But every now and then the top brass at KR set aside a slot
for a smaller paper. *Send someone good,* they would tell
the editor in Grand Forks or Charlotte or Aberdeen. *Your
choice.* Now it was Duluth's turn, with a fellowship available
from mid-January to mid-February of 1991—not a bad time
to be away from northern Minnesota. I let Jodon know of
my interest, and then I sat back and waited for the door to
swing wide. Surely he would give this to me. I had been a
reporter now for more than five years. I had been to Russia, and despite missing all my deadlines there, my stories
had been pretty good and had won some awards. And it was
abundantly clear that I was starting to get restless. At Duke,
I could study fiction writing and history; I could broaden
my horizons; I could come back recharged, bringing news of
the outside world to isolated, snowbound Duluth.

I researched the Raleigh-Durham-Chapel Hill area,
looked up pictures of Duke's green and grassy quad and
imposing stone buildings, learned how to pronounce
Krzyzewski, the crazy last name of the basketball coach
(who everybody just called Coach K) . . . and then Jodon
offered the fellowship to Chris Thompson.

Laurie doesn't always get what she wants, I reminded
Pam in a letter. I acted nonchalant, but I was deeply disap-
pointed. I still loved the *News-Tribune,* I still loved reporting, but I was starting to understand why reporters cycled
through with such regularity. Our newsroom was much
smaller than those at big-city dailies, and resources—and
aspirations—were modest by comparison. Big Sunday sto-

ries were reported and written in two days; there was no time to think, let alone think big. My father's curious praise—"It's remarkable that you can write so quickly and with so much authority"—had begun to sound less like praise and more like a veiled criticism of how slight my work was. I had begun to understand the steady exodus from Duluth. Doubt was starting to replace my cheerful confidence; I was beginning to see how much better I could be—or, more honestly, how mediocre I was. And I despaired of improving while working at such a steady trot.

Chris Thompson turned the fellowship down. His wife was pregnant, and he didn't want to be away from home. You could practically see me swell at this news; I was like the obnoxious kid in the front row whose hand shot into the air at every question from the teacher. *Oh! Me! Pick me! Me!* I didn't have a pregnant wife—all I had was a dog. *Oh, me! Me!* And Jodon, God bless him, picked me.

My apartment in Durham was cozy, with a small bedroom, a kitchenette, and a round wooden table with two ladder-back chairs. This is where I set up the brand-new word processor that I had lugged through three airports. (It was always very complicated getting anywhere from Duluth.) It had a narrow screen that showed six lines of type at a time and a molded plastic carrying case that closed with a firm *snap*. My short stories were stored on little diskettes. No more retyping them all from scratch; now I just popped in a disk, and the story printed out automatically. Amazing. So fast. I could send out hundreds of identical copies, to every literary journal in the country! All I had to do now was write them. Always a great believer in taping things to walls, I taped up some pictures next to the table, to make myself feel at home—postcards, mainly, but also a picture of Toby, and one of my desk back in the newsroom—and propped a black-and-white photo of my hero, E. B. White, next to my computer.

There were seven of us fellows—five from the United States and Canada, and two from Japan—each in an identical apartment in our cube-shaped building, which was built around a central courtyard, its flowers brown and dead this time of year. In my apartment, the single-pane windows rattled in the January wind, and when the electric heat clicked on, a circuit breaker tripped, and I had to crawl out of bed in the chilly dark and flip it back. But I wasn't complaining. In Duluth, my friends were struggling through snowdrifts and twenty-below windchills and pounding out the same old cop stories, city council stories, and business briefs. Here in North Carolina I needed no more than a jacket for the walk to campus—a few blocks along the street and then a convoluted path through the Duke hospitals. I pushed past doctors and visitors and, who knows, brilliant researchers from around the world who were on the verge of incredible discoveries, hurried down the bright, antiseptic halls, and emerged into a serene green quad crisscrossed by walking paths and surrounded by imposing stone buildings. It looked like every episode of *Masterpiece Theater* I had ever seen, and I never got tired of wandering into the chapel, with its soaring ceiling and stained-glass windows, or strolling the quad, staring at the students in what I hoped wasn't a stalkerlike fashion, wondering how it was that they all had the smarts and the wherewithal to be enrolled in such a beautiful and impressive place.

I was issued a Duke University ID badge with a picture of my thrilled, beaming face on it, which allowed me run of the campus. I could sit in on any class I was interested in, browse the libraries, borrow books, attend school events. In return, we were obligated to attend one fellows luncheon a week and make ourselves available to students who might be interested in learning more about our profession. That last requirement was easy for me; the other fellows were from venerable places—the Canadian Broadcasting Corporation, the *New York Times*, the *Washington Post*, and *Time* magazine—and if students wanted a guest speaker to come talk about life in journalism, I was fairly certain that they weren't going to waste their time with someone from the *Duluth News-Tribune*. Frank Lynn, the amiable and sharp political writer from the *Times*, was in great demand; he was constantly trotting off to lunch with a student or to a talk with a dorm group. Dennis Trudeau, the CBC anchor from Montreal, also was invited to speak, but one invitation was revoked at the last minute when the students realized that he wasn't from CBS. Me, I was left entirely alone.

On the first full day, I gathered with the other fellows on the chapel steps for a tour of the campus. Dennis's thick white hair and expensive trench coat set him apart as a television journalist; the rest of us looked fairly frumpy, as I recall, though Frank Lynn was wearing a suit. "What's downtown Durham like?" I asked our tour guide, a blonde senior who was a member of the campus group Dukes and Duchesses. My question surprised her. "I've never been there," she said. "When we go out, we mostly go to Chapel Hill." This struck me as strange; Duke was in Durham, and it seemed singularly lacking in curiosity—not to mention civic pride—to never visit the downtown even once in four years. I made plans to explore it as soon as possible.

I got permission to sit in on a fiction class taught by

Melissa Lentricchia, and another taught by Reynolds Price, who spun around in front of the class in his wheelchair and told stories.

Someone gave me the phone number of the writer Lee Smith, who was teaching in Chapel Hill that semester, and I forced myself to call her up. I listened to the phone ring, and I thought how odd it was that the great Lee Smith, author of *Fair and Tender Ladies*, which I had read three times, and *Me and My Baby View the Eclipse*, which I had two copies of, just in case, had an ordinary telephone that anyone could call. And then someone answered, and I heard, "It's for you!" shouted off into the house somewhere, and I marveled that someone could be so cavalier about living with Lee Smith and answering her phone. Even though I had called up hundreds of important people in my work as a newspaper reporter—mayors, and fire chiefs, and beauty queens, and Governor Rudy Perpich, and, once, Gerard Mulligan, the head writer for the David Letterman show—I was as shy as a groupie while waiting for Lee Smith to come to the phone. I wasn't calling her in my ironclad all-business, just-doing-my-job trappings of a reporter; I was calling her as a student and an admirer.

She put me instantly at ease. She said, "I know Joe Maiolo!" when I told her about my studies at UMD. "He's a good dancer!" She said, "Let's have lunch," and I managed to say, "OK."

Every morning, before anything else, even before coffee, I padded barefoot the six steps from the bed to the word processor, unsnapped the case, and started writing. Without Toby to walk or a newspaper to read or my job to prepare for, I had no early-morning distractions, and I found that this was what I most wanted to do. I was working on a short story called "Snapshots," about a woman who wanted to see her children settled in life before she died, even knowing that everything would blow apart again once she was gone. Although it was set in Minnesota, the story was taking on an oddly Southern flavor, I guess absorbing the North Carolina air I was breathing and the scent of the loblolly pines swaying outside my windows, and I secretly planned to somehow force Lee Smith to read it.

Working on "Snapshots" became the most important part of the first weeks of my fellowship; I grew to love the rhythm of those days. I didn't plan to write first thing in the morning; it just happened—that was when I felt most inspired and diligent, before the rest of the world intruded. Here in Durham, surrounded by brilliant professors and writers and intelligent students and storied halls of learning, the world at my feet, what I craved most was solitude. The hours zipped by, and by early afternoon I was all written out, and I would get dressed and head over to campus.

Amy Goldstein, the fellow from the *Washington Post*, lived across the hall from me, and we became good friends. Sometimes in the evenings we would wrap up in blankets and sit out in the chilly dead courtyard and talk about our lives. Like me, Amy was short and had curly hair, but unlike me, she was intensely focused. She was using her fellowship to study health care policy, which would be her new beat when she returned to Washington. Me, I was using the fellowship broadly, to taste the world. In the evenings, I explored Durham, driving my rental car slowly past white shotgun houses, past empty tobacco sheds, to the quiet downtown. I found a bookstore called Bell Book and Coffee,

....

which hosted public readings in the evenings, and I boldly signed up to come back and read one of my stories. My first public reading. It felt less intimidating doing this in Durham, where I knew not a soul, than in Duluth, where God knows if I would ever have the courage.

Melissa Lentricchia did not want me in her class. Learning to write and critique fiction, she said, requires trust, and she wanted her class to be a tight and cohesive group. Having me swoop in for four weeks and then swoop out again would be disruptive. I saw her point, but four weeks was all I had, and I was determined not to squander it. So I continued to show up, day after day, doing the assignments and trying to act like I belonged. She looked unhappy every time I walked through the door, but she also did me an enormous favor by pointing out another student and suggesting that we might become friends. Marjorie Hudson was tall, with a friendly smile and curly black hair. Like me, she was not a traditional Duke student but a professional, a copy editor at Algonquin Books in Chapel Hill. She had a slow drawl, a quick wit, and an excellent eye for story. She invited me to her house for dinner, down in Pittsboro, along twisty rural roads through dark woods. We made a day of it, making rubbings of old gravestones and volunteering to be part of a church brigade that was clearing underbrush from an overgrown, long-forgotten African American cemetery; her church had been segregated a hundred years before, and so had been its graveyard. She and her daughter and I spent hours cutting back growth and hauling branches, but by late afternoon we had not accomplished much. That lush Carolina undergrowth was not letting go easily, and many of the headstones had been toppled or stolen. We ate dinner at her farmhouse, where she and her husband grew herbs for the chic restaurants of Chapel Hill, and where she worked on her own poetry and fiction. After dinner, Marjorie sat near the woodstove, a blanket over her lap, rocking slowly, and I sat on the floor and scratched the ears of her old golden retriever, Bean; he reminded me of Toby, my golden boy, and it made me homesick. As we talked about our favorite writers, the wind came up, and it began to rain.

Working at Algonquin, Marjorie was steeped in southern writers. I was more of a northern girl, and this whole lush world was somewhat new to me. Marjorie was generous in her enthusiasm. "You have got to read Jill McCorkle, she's too funny," she said. "And Clyde Edgerton. I'll give you *Walking across Egypt.* I give everybody *Walking across Egypt.*"

I tried to think of some northern writers I could offer her in exchange—Louise Erdrich? Garrison Keillor? Tim O'Brien?—but she had already read them all. And then I drove back to Durham in a thunderstorm, the rain lashing my rental car, branches whipping at my windshield. I took the curves slow, and I thought how much I loved it there, how much I already felt at home. It was the first time I had seriously considered that I might be happy living somewhere else.

"This was a scary thing Knight-Ridder did in allowing me to be here like this," I wrote to Pam. "I'm not going to come home 'refreshed and invigorated,' as Jodon suggested; I'm going to come home completely frustrated with my job and ready to quit."

A few days later, Tom Morgan called me from Duluth. He was clearly discouraged. He had dreamed up the brilliant scheme for Mayme Sevander to teach Russian in Duluth and write her memoirs, but as it turned out, there was a flaw in his plan: Mayme could not write. She had not even attempted a memoir, as she and the publisher had discussed, but instead had tried to compile a record of every American Finn ever to immigrate to Petrozavodsk and die in Stalin's purges. Tom told me that her manuscript was not much more than a list of names, padded with random memories in no particular order. She had turned it in and returned to Russia, assuming her book would be in the stores by Christmas, but it would not be. It could not be published. "We need somebody to rewrite it for her," Tom said. "Somebody has to make sense of her story and tell it like a tale. What she's written is unreadable. It would be easier if it was somebody who already knows her, maybe somebody who's already been to Petrozavodsk." I knew what he was asking of me, or I hoped I did, and while the wind rattled the windows and my circuit breaker shut off for the fiftieth time, I sat in the dark listening to Tom's plans, and my heart beat faster. Perhaps my fellowship would have a focus after all.

By the time Tom hung up, I had already started compiling lists in my head of things I needed to do. If I were to write Mayme's story, I would need to learn much more about the immigration of Finns, both to the United States and to the Soviet Union. Surely there were records of this somewhere, and information about Oscar Corgan, Mayme's father. I needed to know more about Russian history in general and Stalin's purges in specific. I needed to find someone on campus who could give me guidance. In the Duke library I found reference to two academics at the Institute of Migration Studies (and who even knew there was such a thing?) in Turku, Finland. Both had written extensively on the Karelian Fever movement, though most of their work was in Finnish, not English. It only took me a day or two after that to track down Dr. Stefan Pugh, who taught Slavic studies at Duke and was an expert in the Karelian language. Let it be known that Stefan Pugh, in one fifteen-minute conversation, changed my life, and he was entirely matter-of-fact about it.

"Next year is the seventy-fifth anniversary of Finland's independence," Dr. Pugh told me. "I think the government is funding some research trips. You could probably get some money and go to Finland to do some research." He said this casually, as though getting a grant and jetting off to Finland were something that a person might do on any day of the week. Could I do that? Was that really possible? He rooted around in his desk drawer and came out with a card. "Here, write to this woman. She's with the Finnish consulate in Washington, D.C. She might be interested in your project." And he jotted down a name and an address.

That evening, I called the city desk and talked to Al Miller, the city editor. I wanted to float the idea of taking a leave, but even before I broached it, he told me that the paper was over budget, and Jodon was looking to save money by offering unpaid leaves of absence over the summer. I hung up thoughtfully. Everything was coming together so nicely you could practically hear it click into place. An opportunity to write a book. A publisher ready to publish it. The possibility of a grant from the government of Finland. Time away from work.

I picked up the phone again and called my friend Tom, a copy editor on the night desk. By now I was so excited my voice was shaking. "Tom, guess what! I'm going to take a six-month leave of absence, and go to Finland, and go back to Russia, and write a book!" There was a pause on the other end, and I could picture Tom raising one eyebrow in that supercilious way of his, and in that pause, that one little moment, all of the things that had started troubling me about Duluth came rolling back. The vastness of Duke, the great sense of possibility, the wonderful feeling that the world was my oyster—was *anybody's* oyster, everybody's oyster—began to shrivel.

"Hmmm," Tom said, with great skepticism. "Nice work, if you can get it."

As I hung up the phone, I thought, *This is why I have to get away. This is why I cannot stay there the rest of my life.*

·

Back to Russia

···

MAYME AND I SAT IN THE GRASSY YARD OF BROOKS
Anderson's Park Point home, and while gulls screeched in
the blueness above our heads, she broke my heart. In her
clipped and decisive way, she told me that she did not want
me to write her book.

Everything had been arranged. Since my return from
Duke, Bob Jodon had agreed to give me a six-month leave of
absence (far longer than the leaves he had initially offered).
Tom Morgan had negotiated with Don Tubesing of Pfeifer-
Hamilton Publishers to not cancel Mayme's book contract,
but instead to consider a new manuscript—one written by
me—in six months' time. And then he had secured a grant
from the Duluth Superior Community Foundation to pay
me $12,000 to write it. He had also found me an office and
a computer at his college, where I could work in near–Ivy
League splendor. The Finnish consulate had come through
as well, and the government of Finland had approved a
grant that would get me to Turku for two weeks of research
at the Institute of Migration Studies. Morgan secured
money that would then get me to Petrozavodsk and back.

Everything was in place, all the complicated arrangements settled in record time. But when Tubesing wrote to

Mayme, telling her that I was coming to Russia in mid-June
to interview her, he used the unfortunate phrase "and to get
inside your soul," and Mayme rebelled. "Absolutely not," she
said. Within days, she had hitched a ride on a trip to Vermont (Vermont and Karelia were sister states) and called
Brooks Anderson from Montpelier, demanding that he get
her to Duluth. Somehow, he did. And now she and I were
sitting in front of his house, a sweet June breeze wafting
off Lake Superior, while my dream of going back to Russia
and writing a book evaporated. What was it that my copy
editor friend had said? *Nice work, if you can get it.* I looked
at Mayme helplessly.

"Don Tubesing says you want to get inside my soul,"
she said, her voice clipped and cold. "No one gets inside my
soul." And I understood her objection. Mayme had no interest in revealing the intimacies of her life. The manuscript
that she had produced in her nine months in Duluth had
not been a memoir, as Morgan and Tubesing had wanted.
She had a grander vision: a record of all the American Finns
who had been murdered in Stalin's purges. It was, in some
way, an attempt to atone for her father, who had unwit-
tingly persuaded hundreds to emigrate to their doom. But
Tubesing wasn't about to publish that grander vision. One
person's tale would sell; a long list of difficult Finnish names
would not. He and Morgan had met with Mayme a day or
two before to tell her that. She needed to decide: book, or no
book? It was up to her.

And so I changed the subject. I didn't argue; argu-
ing with Mayme was a waste of oxygen. Instead, I set my
pocket-sized tape recorder in the grass in front of her and
asked her to tell me about growing up in Superior. Mayme
picked up the tape recorder and examined it with curios-

ity, clicking the buttons off and on and flipping open the cover to watch the microcassette whir. "This could be very handy," she said. "If I thought of something in the middle of the night, when you're not around, I could record it for you."

"It's yours," I said immediately. Replacing my tape recorder would be a small price indeed for Mayme's cooperation.

In the five years since the sister-city visit, Russia had grown shabby. From the window of my snug compartment on the Helsinki–Leningrad train, I watched glorious Finnish fields of golden rapeseed give way to dark Russian forests. We passed tidy Finnish train stations, freshly painted in blue and white and cheery with planters of blooming geraniums. Across the border, we chugged past concrete monstrosities with cracked platforms and shabby station houses, each topped by a red star. At one stop I watched from the window as a man crawled out of the weeds toward the tracks, a bottle in one hand.

Mayme never told me that she had changed her mind about her book. But for two weeks she met with me daily, talking at length about life in Superior in the 1930s and about her father's work, first editing a Finnish-language newspaper and, later, traveling the upper Midwest, giving speeches at Finn Halls, recruiting settlers for Stalin's Russia. Her oldest brother had died before the family emigrated, and when she spoke of him, she wept, and I nervously waited for her to regain her composure. I did not think she would want me to acknowledge her distress, this tough, proud woman, so I stayed quiet, pretending to read over my notes until she was able to speak.

I spent two weeks in Turku, interviewing the scholars

at the Institute for Migration Studies and going through
their files, photocopying newspaper clippings and other
documents to mail home for translation. And then I took
the train back to Russia. In Petrozavodsk, private commerce
had come out into the open. The wide main street was lined
with stalls where merchants sold all kinds of things—stack
ing dolls painted to look like Gorbachev and Reagan, gold-
trimmed religious icons that once were available only in
berioska shops, and original artwork that satirized the
political system. One man sold individual sticks of Wrig-
ley's Juicy Fruit gum, each stick torn neatly in half. The
Hotel Sevarnaya had fallen into disrepair; most of the tiles
had come off the wall in my bathroom and were piled in a
crooked stack on the floor. But the same fierce babushka
glowered at me from her station in the hallway, demanding
my room key every time I left and retrieving it for me, muttering, upon my return. The Soviet Union was on the verge
of collapse, but it still had full employment.

Every morning, Stella Sevander came by my hotel, and
we set out to talk with another old American Finn: Vieno
Levanen of Massachusetts; Sirkka Rikka of Detroit; Ruth
Niskanen of Palo, Minnesota; Erwin and Elsie Niva, one
from Minnesota, one from South Dakota; Otto Bjorinen of
Michigan; Ernest Haapaniemi from the Copper Country
of Hancock, Michigan; Mayme's brother, Paul Corgan, and
her little sister Aino. All told essentially the same story,
the story I had heard at Mayme's apartment five years earlier. Only this time the stories were punctuated with sad,
hard details about discrimination, deprivation, and death.
They had been young children in the 1920s and 1930s when
their parents uprooted their families, sold the farms, quit

their jobs, and moved to the Soviet Union, hauling sewing machines and plows and tools and other supplies with them. Brass bands played, and banners snapped in the breeze as their ships steamed away from New York Harbor, and all was festive and merry. But once in Communist Russia, their passports were confiscated, and the families dispatched to Petrozavodsk to live in primitive communal barracks with dozens of other families. With their tools, money, and expertise, the Finns built the modern city of Petrozavodsk—its roads and schools, its plumbing and sidewalks. This work was done in their spare time, on Saturdays, through unpaid community projects called *Subbotniks*.

After a few years, Stalin closed the world up around them. They were forbidden from speaking Finnish; their schools and newspapers were closed; they were not allowed to travel; they were forced out of work. Because they were foreign-born, they were viewed with suspicion. And then came the knock at the door, at night—always at night. The fathers disappeared, and the mothers and children—now family members of an Enemy of the People—were banished into exile, where many of them starved. Ruth Niskanen's mother had nothing to eat but grass, and she died. I heard this story over and over, two and three times a day, told in eloquent detail by stoic, round-faced Finns who, by rights, were still American citizens but who had not seen their homes for sixty years and had no chance of ever seeing them again. I began to understand Mayme's fervor to collect and publish their names. She wanted them to be remembered, every one of them. I opened my notebook and jotted what became the opening line of our book: "My story is one of many . . ."

One afternoon, Stella's husband, Igor, arranged to take me to Kotkozero to interview an elderly Finnish woman named Elsa Mikkonen. He pulled up at my hotel a half hour late; the gas station had had no gasoline that morning, he explained, so he had traded two bottles of vodka for a tankful of jet fuel. As we bumped down the narrow forest road, I noticed that his car had no windshield wipers; he laughed and explained that he kept them tucked under his front seat. If you leave them on the car, he said, people will steal them. We drove a long distance along a tar road that cut through towering pine forests, passing occasional clearings where I glimpsed groups of women in head scarves bent over vegetable patches, hacking at the ground with hoes. "Is that a communal farm?" I asked, and Igor looked at me with amusement. "No," he said. "Just vegetable gardens at country dachas."

Kotkozero was not much more than a village, with dusty dirt roads and a statue of Lenin, eternally pointing. I waited in the car while Igor inquired at the shop for directions to Elsa Mikkonen's house. A woman in knee-high rubber boots pumped past on an ancient bicycle; a cow grazed in the shade of a tree. Igor was gone a long time, and I grew sleepy. "Elsa was inside the shop, buying bread," he said when he returned. "I had to talk her into being interviewed. She is very shy. We'll meet her at her house." And he started up the Lada.

Elsa was a tiny woman of seventy-one with thin gray hair and a squint that made her appear pleasantly befuddled. She lived alone in one room of a large green house surrounded by birch trees. After greeting us shyly, she lugged her battered tin kettle down the hall, filled it with water for tea, and hoisted it onto her hot plate, and then she settled in her rocking chair and began to talk. Her parents were immigrants from Finland, settling in Cape Cod, Massachusetts. Her father, Armas, lost his laborer job during the Great Depression, and her mother, Helen, took in washing and mending to keep the family alive. After more than a year out of work, Armas—already a strong Socialist—began looking to the Soviet Union, attracted by the promise of full employment and free health care. Helen, homesick for Finland, was drawn by the proximity of Soviet Karelia to her homeland.

The family left Cape Cod for Russia in 1933. On their last night in America, their friends threw a party for them at the local Finn Hall. Inside all was feasting and merriment, but outside one of her uncles stood watch all night with a shotgun. "These were the days of the Red Scare," Elsa said. "The Ku Klux Klan had burned a cross on a Communist's lawn not too long before."

In Russia, the Mikkonens were sent to live in Uhtua, a Finnish-speaking community deep in the forests of northern Karelia, very near the Finnish border. Elsa and her brother fished in the river and collected berries in birchbark baskets. Uhtua—now known as Kalevala—was more Finnish than Russian. Elsa attended a Finnish-speaking school, and her parents read Finnish-language newspapers. Their life was simple and, at times, hard, but they were happy to be back, everything so familiar, so close to home.

"And then they began to arrest people," Elsa said, and she rocked a little faster. "Every night they took someone from Uhtua. It was terrible." Elsa and her family survived the purges, though they were sent into exile. But her uncle was arrested. "Years later, I got a certificate of death. It said—I cried when I got it—it said, 'Execution by shooting squad.' The Finns were all shot. We were all enemies. That's what we were."

She rocked faster, and faster, and then stopped.

In 1955, Elsa was sent to teach in Kotkozero, about fifty miles outside of Petrozavodsk. She never married, never traveled. She lived in that remote Russian village and taught English, and that was her life for the next forty years. She told me all of this simply, with an air almost of bewilderment. Her whole life had been controlled by others—her parents taking her to Russia, the authorities first sending her into exile, then bringing her back and determining what she would study, what she would teach, where she would live. But she was not bitter. She spoke of Cape Cod wistfully; she wished that she might see it again, but she knew that she would not. "I'm too old and too crippled," she said. "My time is done. This is my home now. This is my fatherland. I was once an American. I was once a Finn. But I am Russian now."

Elsa cried when she told me this story, and I felt my throat tighten as I watched her rock so fiercely in that big chair, looking so small and sad and old. When I stood to leave, she took my hand and pressed it warmly. "I was afraid to talk to you, a journalist from America," she said. "But now I see that you are just a simple girl."

On July 4, Stella invited me to her apartment. A flowered cloth covered the dining room table, which was loaded with food—sausage rolls, tomatoes and sour cream, brown bread, cake and tea. A small group of American Finns had been invited—Ruth Niskanen, and Mayme's brother, sister, and son. We ate and chatted, and then Stella brought out a cassette player. "You must be sad to be away from your country on this important holiday," she said. She pressed *play*, and the tape started up. First I heard the rough whirring of the motor, then the warm hiss of the tape, and then Barbra Streisand's impossibly clear voice filled the room. She was singing "God Bless America." And one by one, the American Finns, trapped for their entire lives inside the Soviet regime, joined in.

As my month abroad drew to a close, I began to worry about the logistics of getting home. Soviet bureaucracy being what it was, I could not buy a train ticket in Petrozavodsk that would take me back to Finland; I could only buy a ticket as far as Leningrad. Once there, I must find my way to the Hotel Moskva, which had a travel office where I could buy the Helsinki ticket, and then I must get from the hotel to Finland Station. All this without speaking the language or knowing my way around the city. And I must not miss my connection, because my visa was within hours of expiring.

I worried the whole way back to Leningrad, the whole twelve hours on the train. I lay awake in my berth, listening to the rhythmic rattle as we hurtled down the tracks, feeling the train shudder to a stop at small stations along the way, working in my mind how I was going to get out of the country. In Leningrad, I hopped down from the train, my very American-looking purple and black nylon duffle bag in one hand, my olive green drawstring bag in the other, and hailed what appeared to be a taxi. Amazingly, it stopped. "Hotel Moskva," I said. The driver looked at me. He said something, I didn't know what. I repeated, with something like desperation, "Hotel Moskva."

He took me there, careening through the streets of
lovely Leningrad, down broad Nevsky Prospekt, into the
parking lot of the gargantuan concrete hotel. I leaped out
of the cab and did my best to pantomime that I needed him
to wait, tossed him a package of Marlboros, then dashed
into the hotel, down the long corridor, somehow found the
tourist office, and pushed open the door. It was packed with
people, and the ticket window was closed. My visa, my visa
. . . it expired at midnight. I needed to get to Finland. The
ticket window slid open. A woman looked out and said,
first in Russian, and then in halting English, that the tourist
office would reopen in one half hour. The window slammed
shut. The waiting people didn't move. They lounged against
the wall, on chairs, in the doorway, smoking, chatting dully.
They looked as though they had already been there for a
long time. I paced. I must not miss that train. I watched
the minutes tick past. I ran back out to the parking lot to
check on my cab. He was patiently waiting. I waved at him,
ran back inside. The hour ticked past the promised opening time, but the window remained shut. I boldly opened
the door to the back room and poked my head inside. Three
clerks sat drinking tea. "I need to get a ticket!" I said. They
hollered at me in Russian, and I slammed the door.

Finally, the window slid open once again, and the waiting travelers surged forward. There was no orderly line,
just chaos, everyone shoving everyone else, trying to get
to the front. The crowd smelled of sweat and cigarettes. I
decided that the only way to succeed was to become Russian. I pushed and shoved and elbowed my way to the window. I didn't care who I knocked over. I needed to get out
of the country! Panting and disheveled, I suddenly found
myself at the window, the clerk staring at me impassively.

I ordered my ticket ("Helsinki," I said, over and over, and she painstakingly wrote it out in longhand). I grabbed it and fled. "Finland Station! Finland Station!" I gasped to the cabbie. (I was getting pretty good at speaking only in frantic nouns.) I showed him my ticket and hoped he understood. He took me to the station and dumped me at the curb. I hauled out my bags; poking out of the top of the drawstring were the bristles of a straw broom that I had bought the day before in the Petrozavodsk farmers' market, and an empty Pepsi bottle marked with Cyrillic writing. (Clearly, I had not improved at buying souvenirs.) I paid the driver and tossed a couple of packages of Marlboros onto the front seat, and he pulled away so fast he almost ran over my foot. And then I just—stopped. I had reached my limit; I could practically feel the adrenaline ebbing from my body. I stared at all of the people hurrying in and out of the station, knowing exactly where they were going, the hands on the big clock tower sweeping down the minutes to my unknown departure time. I couldn't read my ticket, couldn't read any of the signs, couldn't ask anybody any questions. Here I was, obstacles surmounted, documents in hand, destination achieved, unable to go any farther. I realized that I was exhausted. A man approached. He was tall and well dressed, wearing expensive-looking snakeskin cowboy boots. He said, "Do you need a porter?" A porter! A porter was a luxury, something a fur-clad Westerner carrying a dog with a jeweled collar might require. But then I felt something crumple inside of me—I think it was relief—and I said, almost recklessly, "Yes."

The man picked up my duffle bag and moved three steps forward. And then he stopped and set it back down. "We wait," he said. And we waited, for what felt like a long time.

After a while I looked at him anxiously, and he said, again, "We wait."

I reached into my pocket and fingered my last few notes of Russian money. What would a porter charge? What would be an appropriate tip? I was almost broke, and I still had three days in Helsinki before my flight home. People rushed past. The clock ticked, ticked. Finally the man picked up my bag and began to walk briskly toward the tracks. I slung my drawstring bag onto my shoulder, the stiff broom bristles scratching my neck, and trotted after him. He had not asked me any questions—not where I was going, not what train I was on, not anything. He walked halfway down the tracks and set down my bag. He said, "We wait." After a long while a train chugged in, and I watched people disembark, flowing past me, and dozens more stream out of the station, climbing the metal steps to their cars. The stranger did not move. When I looked at him, he did not return the look but only smiled into space.

Questions flooded my mind. Was he really a porter? He seemed awfully well dressed and urbane for such a job. Did he know Stella? Had she asked him to look out for me? I remembered a story that Tom Morgan had told me about his first trip to Russia, years and years ago when he was still in college. He and his wife had made a day of it in the countryside, and late that night as they waited at a rural train station, he turned to her and said, "I hope the train to Moscow stops here this late." And the man who had been following them all day stepped out of the shadows and said, "It does," and stepped back again. Was my porter KGB? I looked at him again, and something about his demeanor stopped me from asking him anything.

After a while, the man said, "Your ticket, please," and I handed it to him. It was handwritten in ink on coarse grayish paper. He walked down the tracks and handed it to the babushka who waited by the train. They spoke, and then he walked back, picked up my duffle bag, and said, "Follow me."

By now I was fingering every ruble note I had in my pockets. Would he expect a huge tip? He had gotten me to the train, waited with me for a considerable amount of time, and negotiated with the babushka—surely this was worth my remaining forty rubles and all of my Marlboros. I followed him onto the train and down the narrow corridor. He pushed open a compartment door and stuffed my bag onto the high shelf, and then he ducked back out the door and walked away. I poked my head out of the doorway. "Wait! Wait!" I said, and he turned and looked at me. Foolishly, I held up my hands. I clutched ruble notes in one, packages of Marlboros in the other. The man in the snakeskin boots smiled gently and shook his head. He said, "Have a good trip."

I came back from Russia in late July and settled into my borrowed office in Tower Hall, a room so large and empty that when the phone rang I heard an echo. I had a desk and a computer and two big windows that gave me a view of Lake Superior. I taped some postcards to the wall, and a picture of Toby, and got to work. Writing a book at the College of St. Scholastica proved to be an entirely different experience than writing stories in the newsroom. Tower Hall might have been noisy and chaotic when classes were in session, but on hot afternoons in late July the summer light filtered through yellowed shades, the dim hallways were cool and quiet, the occasional nun whispered past. Every morning I woke with the sun, walked Toby, and then followed the path through the woods to the college. I shut my office door so that I could concentrate, and I wrote. Around ten o'clock Mayme would burst through, checking up on me and occasionally making demands. ("There is a sale on bras at the Glass Block! Bring your car around at two!") She knew that I needed her cooperation to get this book done, and I knew it too; I was accommodating and obedient, in order to keep her talking, and willingly served as her part-time chauffeur. Some days, though, I grew weary of her and locked my door. If she would only knock, I thought, I would let her in. But she never would. I could hear her trying the handle again and again, and then clipping off down the hall. And I would quietly unlock the door, ashamed of my pettiness.

I had not considered, when I had taken this assignment, that writing something the length of a book was entirely different from any kind of writing I had done before. I wrote the first chapter in record time, all in one morning, and then did a word count. Hmmmm. About a thousand words, the length of one full column of type in a newspaper. Clearly not enough. Now what? *More detail. I need more detail.* This was going to be harder than I had thought.

Despite those abrupt morning appearances, having Mayme around was invaluable. I spent a couple of hours every day interviewing her, meshing her memories with the memories I had collected from her friends in Petrozavodsk, and giving her drafts of chapters to read as I completed them. When the memories disagreed, as they occasionally did, I consulted Don Tubesing. "This is Mayme's story," he said. "Go with her version."

All summer I walked around with Mayme's brisk voice inside my head. She was fluent in English but spoke with a British inflection and used dated idioms, which I, too, began to use without thinking: *He was knee-high to a grasshopper! They got along like a house afire!* I could summon her voice anytime I wanted to and sometimes when I didn't want to; at times, it felt like Mayme was taking over my brain.

I missed the noisy camaraderie of the newsroom, the constant jokes, the shouts across the cubicles, the liveliness of people coming and going all day and all night, talking about their stories and interviews, that intensity of working on deadline. At Scholastica, every few hours I would look up from my work and listen . . . and hear nothing except, occasionally, the quiet tread of a professor climbing the weathered staircase outside my door. I wished for someone to talk to, someone to laugh with. But I didn't have a lot of time to waste; the deadline was a constant anxiety. Pfeifer-Hamilton now needed the manuscript completed by November, a month earlier than planned, and so I stared out at the lake for a while and then returned to my work.

I had no computer at home—just that funny little word processor that I had lugged to Duke—and sometimes after dinner I walked back to the college to do some more work. On those evenings, I took Toby with me, for company on the dark walk home through the woods. I smuggled him up a remote staircase of Tower Hall to the third floor and into my office, where he slept at my feet while I typed, a sweet presence in that solitude. When we heard a noise—a late-night professor, a janitor, who knows?—he raised his head and looked at me. "Shhhh," I said, and he lay back down. It occurred to me that that summer I had come close to achieving my high school dream of living in the woods and writing; the difference, of course, was that instead of a posse of cats, I had Toby, which was so much better.

Joey was visiting from the Twin Cities one summer day, when the phone rang. The woman on the other end said that her name was Rachel and that she was calling from the North Carolina Writers Network, and she seemed to be telling me that I had won something. In my confusion, I did my best to get her off the phone; I was trying to talk to Joey, and I thought the caller was a telephone scammer. But she was persistent, and it slowly dawned on me what she was talking about: that short story I had written at Duke, "Snapshots," the story with the oddly North Carolina flavor. Lee Smith had read it for me, and she had liked it. She had made a couple of suggestions ("How about saying simply, 'and he was crying' here? Single tears seem fake to me," she had written in the margin) but mostly had been encouraging. ("I think this story is just wonderful, Laurie," she scrawled in pencil on the last page. "A real pleasure to read, both intelligent *and* moving.") And so I had boldly entered it in the Thomas Wolfe Fiction competition and then had forgotten all about it. And now this woman, this very nice woman, this wonderful, wonderful Rachel, was telling me that I had won. (And was thinking, I found out later, "Who is Laurie Hertzel? And where is Duluth?") But the news was delightful: the judge had been Anne Tyler; the prize was five hundred dollars.

Mayme returned to Russia in August, and so began the laborious and time-consuming process of printing out new chapters, packing them up, writing letters studded

with questions, mailing the whole bundle off to Petrozavodsk, and then waiting for her response. Tower Hall grew
busier with the return of the faculty for fall semester, and I
began venturing out of my office to eat lunch with some of
the English professors. They were friendly and welcoming
and seemed curious, in a bemused sort of way, about how,
exactly, one collaborates with Mayme Sevander on a book
project. They had spent a year around Mayme when she was
teaching with Tom Morgan, and they knew her very well.

I began to like the quiet, thoughtful atmosphere more
and more, and I wondered if there was some way I could
make a more permanent leap from the newsroom to a college. Truth be told, I hadn't thought this through; I wasn't so
much interested in the teaching aspect as in the writing-all-
day-in-my-private-office aspect and then hanging around
with the faculty. My friend Marjorie wrote from North Carolina that she had enrolled in the long-distance MFA course
at Warren Wilson College and was having a wonderful
time and learning a lot. "It's designed for midcareer pro-
fessionals," she told me. "Most people in the program have
demanding full-time jobs—lots of lawyers. We get together
twice a year for two weeks, and then you do the rest by mail.
You'd love it." But there was that pesky matter of the bach-
elor's degree, still unfinished. Although I had tons of credits, I didn't necessarily have the right credits. I had rather
airily skipped many of the basic requirements—biology,
and astronomy, and whatever the other ones were. I had just
taken the fun stuff—sort of like going to Old Country Buffet
and heading directly for the pudding table. One evening I
got out all of my transcripts, from my year at Scholastica
and from all those odd day and night classes at UMD, and

I toted them up. I had almost enough to meet the requirements of a double-major in English and history and a minor in journalism, but other than testing out of freshman composition, I had almost none of the general ed requirements. I figured I was still at least a full year away from graduating, and it would be a year of all spinach. No pudding. With a full-time job, it would take longer. The degree was getting to be a sore spot with me, a raw annoyance that rubbed at my brain and that I tried to ignore. I should have finished a long time ago, and now I did not want to go back and take Biology 101. I was ready to immerse myself in something—a master's degree, maybe, in creative nonfiction. So I made an appointment with the English department chair at UMD to see if there was some way to finally get this done.

As it happened, the chair of the English department turned out to be someone I had never had for a class. This did not help my case. He and my father knew each other, and this did not help my case either. We met in his small, cluttered office at UMD, and I sat down nervously by his desk. He did not say anything but waited for me to speak. "I'm a reporter for the *News-Tribune*," I explained. "I've been taking classes part-time for years, but now I'm wondering if there's some way to expedite getting a degree so I can go to grad school."

The department head leaned back in his chair and stared at me. He did not look encouraging. He made a tent of his hands and bounced his fingertips together. He allowed me to wait a long time before answering. "I cannot believe how arrogant you are," he said. "You think that education is something that can be speeded up?" This was not the response I had been expecting, and I sucked in my breath. "Going to college is a privilege," he said. "I have students who live on beans and starve in garrets" (at this point my mind began to wander as I tried to picture which houses in Duluth had actual garrets) "in order to stay in school. And you think you can keep your little job and hurry up your degree?"

Bounce bounce bounce went the fingertips.

He told me that if I wanted a degree, then I should quit my job and devote myself to my schooling. After a while I thanked him for his time, and I got up and left. That's it, I told myself. I'm done. I felt equal parts anger and relief. And I knew that it meant that once the Mayme book was written, I was headed back to the *News-Tribune*.

•

The Long Goodbye

....

ONE AFTERNOON AT THE END OF OCTOBER, IT START-
ed to snow. I looked up from the computer and watched the
flakes swirl outside my window in Tower Hall, thicker and
thicker, until the sky was just a blur, cars getting covered,
grass disappearing, the lake in the distance gone, vanished
behind a wall of white, and it occurred to me that if I was
ever going to make it home, I had better leave now. I had
not seen snow like this in years, and never so early; it was
only Halloween. Usually snow in Duluth doesn't stick until
Thanksgiving or so, but this was falling too fast to melt. I
could hear the whine of tires spinning on slick streets, see
people dashing for their cars, coats pulled over their heads.
I grabbed my jacket and ran through the wet flakes into the
woods and along the slippery path to my house. And there
I stayed, for the next three days. The snow fell all day and
all night and all day and all night, and poor Toby had a hard
time churning through it when I pushed open the back door
to let him out. I tried to shovel a little area for him, but the
wind blew the snow back in my face, and, shivering, I called
Toby inside and slammed the door. It stormed without stopping until the third of November. That morning, the skies
began to clear, but by then the snow on the ground was
more than three feet deep.

My street was not plowed for days, but I could not have gone anywhere even if it had been; I had no garage, and my poor Toyota was buried in drifts. That first morning, I tried cross-country skiing up the street and through the woods to get to the college, but I sank in the deep snow, and the long skis were only marginally useful on the hilly path. After that, I pulled on my Carhartt coveralls, laced up my Sorels, and broke trail on snowshoes, arriving at Tower Hall breathing hard and snowy to the knees. Nobody would have mistaken me for an academic.

By now, most of Mayme's book was done, and all that was left was cleanup—fact-checking, revisions, and an afterword. I had written two versions of an epilogue, but Mayme had disliked both, sending them back from Petrozavodsk with a brusque note claiming that she would never say such things, even though I had taken most of the text verbatim from tape-recorded interviews earlier that summer. But the recent collapse of the Soviet Union had changed her attitude about a lot of things—or perhaps had allowed her to publicly state her attitude—and she was no longer comfortable swearing allegiance to the Communist Party as she had been in June.

As my work drew to a close, I wondered what to do next. I had all of December with no obligations, and I was beginning to see that I had some options. Writing the book had made me comfortable with long-form journalism, and so I pitched a story about the American Finns in Russia to the editor of *Minnesota Monthly* in Minneapolis. Len Witt's answer was prompt but blunt, giving no clue how much this exchange would eventually affect me: "It sounds interesting," he said, "but I don't have any idea who you are. How do I know you can pull it off?"

Witt was just being honest, but his answer annoyed me even though he eventually bought the piece; it seemed to sum up the attitude of most Twin Citians about anyone who lived outside of the metro area: *Who are you again? And, Um, Duluth?*

I found myself defending Duluth a lot, even as it became apparent that I was spending a lot of time trying to go just about anywhere else. Over the next year, I busily applied for fellowships, writing workshops, and out-of-town assignments: I was looking around more than I let myself realize. Each time I left, I came back knowing a little more. At a writing conference at Wesleyan University in Connecticut, author George Garrett critiqued my short stories and made it clear how far I had to go by gently suggesting that there was nothing wrong with being known as "the woman who publishes in the *South Carolina Review*." (For, yes, the *South Carolina Review* had accepted a story of mine, which they then accidentally published twice.) Another writer, Richard Bausch, urged those of us at the conference to steal time from ourselves, not from our families or jobs, if we wanted to write. He suggested writing in the middle of the night. "I need my sleep!" one participant said, and Bausch looked at his buddy, David Slavitt, who shrugged. "So don't write," Slavitt said. "Nobody cares." This was disturbing, but I knew it was true: Nobody cares.

Year-long journalism fellowships at Stanford and Michigan were something of a long shot, but I applied anyway, tapping my professor friends for recommendations. Knight-Ridder was looking for a reporter from a regional paper to serve a three-year stint in its Washington bureau, to bring an outside-the-beltway perspective to their coverage. I applied, even though I wasn't sure I wanted to spend three years in D.C. The opportunity I really pinned my hopes on, though, was the Thurber House fellowship in Columbus, Ohio. The Thurber House—James Thurber's childhood home and the setting for his book *My Life and Hard Times*—awarded four fellowships a year, one of them specifically for journalists. This felt like a perfect fit. The fellowship would be three months of nearly uninterrupted writing time; the only obligations were teaching a class at Ohio State University and serving as the writing coach for a small group of reporters at the *Columbus Dispatch*.

Everyone turned me down: Stanford, Michigan, the Thurber House, Knight-Ridder. The rejection note from the Thurber House was so kindly worded, though, with an encouraging "Try us again," that I immediately set about writing a new application for the next round. By now I was very used to not getting things on the first try.

Back in the newsroom that snowy January it became apparent that money was tight. The recession of 1991 was spilling over into 1992, and in response we were churning more positions than ever; that is, the editors put off replacing departing writers, sometimes for months. The news hole had shrunk again, and our features staff was no more—not laid off, but folded into the news staff as it had been when I had started at the paper fifteen years before. Fifteen years! Could it be possible? Still, I had to admit, it was fun to be back. I had missed the atmosphere of the newsroom, so relaxed, yet so intense.

That month, a freelance writer named Ann Bauer pitched a consumer column to the paper. "The Smart Shopper" was meant to be a practical guide to saving money, a natural fit for newspapers during economic hard times. Her first column, which ran in January, was on how to sell a house without using a real estate agent. It seemed an innocuous enough topic, but after it ran, the Realtors were furious. They protested that the column was irresponsible and simplistic. Here they had been pumping advertising into the newspaper for decades, for generations, and now, in their eyes, we had not just insulted them, we had damaged their business by running a column that called them unnecessary. Jodon met with them and apologized, but it was not enough. The Realtors pulled their ads from the Sunday paper and placed them, instead, in one of the weekly shoppers.

In the newsroom, we were both angry and baffled. Journalists are trained to understand that we should pay attention only to the truth and to the news; we should not be swayed by the whims and desires of readers or advertisers. The Ann Bauer column seemed fine to us, but Jodon, the editor, saw it differently. Classifieds were the lifeblood of newspapers; those little ads in the back of the paper paid most of our bills. Automobile ads and help-wanted ads had already taken a big hit with the recession, and now the loss of real estate ads could do us some real harm. Jodon canceled "The Smart Shopper" and offered the Realtors space for a rebuttal. They wrote a column—one in which they claimed that selling one's home without a real estate agent was a folly tantamount to performing brain surgery on one's self—and Jodon wrote a column of his own, apologizing.

Bauer fought back hard. She filed a libel suit against Jodon and the paper (and ultimately lost). She took her case to a columnist at the *Star Tribune* in Minneapolis, who wrote about it, and to a writer at the *Columbia Journalism Review*, who awarded the *News-Tribune* a "dart" in its monthly "darts and laurels" column. She sent her column to an editor at the *Chicago Tribune* and asked him to point out the flaws. The *Chicago Tribune* editor told her there was nothing wrong with it; it was a fine consumer spending column. But "The Smart Shopper" did not run again in the *News-Tribune*. The real estate ads returned after a week or two; there was not yet anywhere else for them to go that commanded the circulation that we had. But their brief departure was a chill warning that the balance of power had started to shift.

Since returning from my leave, I was working just four days a week, using that extra day off for fiction writing and free-lancing. Writing for *Minnesota Monthly* was fun, but it was hard, and it was clear I still had a lot to learn. Len Witt sent back the first big profile I wrote for him with a cryptic note: "This is a great, great newspaper profile," he said. "Now make it a magazine profile." But how, exactly, was I to do that? And what was the difference?

I liked the solitude of this writing life; I liked the focused way I spent my time. I liked being busy. But there were times when I was lonely. Once again, my friends were leaving. Katy moved to New Orleans, taking a job at the *Times-Picayune*. Doug took a job at the *Toledo Blade* and then, a few years later, at the *St. Paul Pioneer Press*. The calm Rott moved to Louisville, and Tom, the copy editor, left for divinity school. Erik was the last straw; my closest friend in recent years, he left for the *San Jose Mercury News*, where Murrell had gone a decade before. I had lived in Duluth my entire life, and you would think that I would have a million friends there, but most of my friends were journalists, and they kept moving on. I went to goodbye party after goodbye party after goodbye party. The people I worked with kept getting younger—no, wait; I was getting older, now in my midthirties. Could I continue to hang around with twenty-somethings when I was in my forties? My fifties? When would it become creepy and weird? I pictured myself as Gordy Behrens, standing at the bar in the Pickwick, picking up the tab.

Later that year Jodon, too, moved on. I wondered why anyone would want to be a top editor; none of them ever stayed more than a few years, fired or summarily transferred by unseen bosses in Miami. His replacement was Vicki Gowler, a short, energetic woman with wild dark curls who had been in Knight-Ridder's Washington bureau. She encouraged me to continue my sob sister stories about social issues. Gay servicemen forced to conceal their sexual orientation, teenage mothers struggling to finish high school and raise their babies, widows trying to make it through that first sad year alone. With Vicki's encouragement, I looked for stories that reflected the drama of everyday life. I wrote about an elderly woman who nearly froze to death in her home because her utilities had been turned off. The mailman had noticed her mail and newspapers piling up on the porch and called police. Her son, whom I tried to interview, called me a vulture and hung up on me. I wrote about a couple that was set to adopt two little girls until the girls' grandmother kidnapped them and hustled them to Texas. And one day I drove to the Stillwater state prison, near the Twin Cities, to interview a man who had murdered his wife.

Stillwater prison was huge and old. Gliding barred doors

separated the high-ceilinged lobby from the echoing cell block. The murderer and I sat alone in the warden's office and talked for three hours. He spent most of the time justifying his crime, telling me in detail of extreme, implausible incidents where he was sure his wife had cheated on him. ("I'm pretty sure she had sex with two or three men that day. And then the next day, I think she had sex with one or two guys that day.") When he spoke of the murder, it was without emotion. He told me about the fatal shot—point-blank to the back of her head—and pantomimed it, making a gun of his index finger and thumb, aiming carefully. "I saw pieces of her brain splatter," he said. "I knew she was dead."

That winter, Vicki gave me a weekly column. It was one more part-time job added to all the part-time jobs I already had: a night GA shift, social issues enterprise stories, coaching writers, and filling in on the city desk as needed. I had no desire to write about myself or my life in the column, though occasionally in a panic I was reduced to that, once writing about my dog when a more significant topic eluded me. I was more interested in telling stories of Duluth life, Sue Willoughby–like tales of people you might pass on the street every day but know nothing about. And so I went with a young gay man to get the results of his AIDS test. I followed a single mother through the impersonal assembly-line process of collecting Christmas toys for her children from the Salvation Army. I wrote about what it was like to live on minimum wage. One afternoon a radio announcer called me up to tell me he had liked that day's column and said he was going to mention it on his show. "I've been reading you since you were hyphenated," he said. But there is balance in all things, and another reader called the same day to tell me that she found my columns naive and self-aggrandizing.

That winter, there had been a sharp increase in gun violence—unusual for Duluth. A lot of the shootings were not fatal, but even an injury would be almost unfathomably awful. I wanted to fathom it. What did it feel like? What damage would it do? How would your life change? So I spent a few hours in the newsroom library, going through crime clips, looking for victims to interview. I had a lot to choose from.

Eventually, I settled on Betty Peterson, who lived along the south shore in Wisconsin. She had been bowling with a boyfriend when her ex-husband walked in, pointed a gun at the back of her head, and pulled the trigger. Then he aimed at the boyfriend and shot him as well. Betty survived; the boyfriend did not. Her ex-husband was someone I had interviewed years ago, when I was on the regional desk: Wayne O. Lowe, city clerk for Washburn, Wisconsin, for more than thirty years. I remembered him as a small man, one whom I, at five feet two, towered over. I found Betty's number and gave her a call. She was friendly and willing to talk, but she was on her way to work—could I call her back the next day?

And that is where I ran into difficulty. The gunshot wound had caused short-term memory problems, so we made appointment after appointment, and she kept forgetting them. It took weeks to hook up with her again. When we finally did talk, she told me everything, in vivid detail. She told me how Wayne had walked into the bowling alley. His hands were hanging straight down at his sides. He held a pistol in his right hand. She turned away, heard a loud noise, and fell. She told me about being in the hospital and about her many surgeries. The doctors inserted a plastic plate in her head to cover the hole left by the bullet.

At night, when she turned over in bed, it crackled. "It wakes me up," she said.

By spring, I felt as though my job was on the verge of changing. It became increasingly clear that Vicki wasn't happy with the four-day schedule I had worked out with Jodon. She wanted Sunday stories from me, which almost always necessitated working Fridays. Sometimes she called me in on short notice to fill in somewhere or to rework a story. More and more, I was working five days, not four. My brother Tommy gave me advice: "If you think your job is going to change, then change it yourself, first," he said. "That way you're in control of what happens." This made sense, but I couldn't think what to suggest; I liked my life the way it was. I didn't want it to change.

And then I got a phone call from Len Witt. *Minnesota Monthly* needed an associate editor, and he asked me if I would consider the job. It didn't sound like a bad job—some editing, some writing, a little calendar-type grunt work. But I turned it down with hardly a thought. My life was here. A few weeks later, he called again. He had a new offer—a similar job but slightly better. He had rejiggered the duties, gotten rid of some of the grunt work. I decided it couldn't hurt to talk, so I drove down to the Twin Cities and interviewed with him and the art director, Mark Shafer. They took me to lunch in downtown Minneapolis, and I scanned the menu for my favorite meal (bacon, lettuce, and tomato sandwich), but, sadly, it wasn't listed. Other things were, mysterious other things. *What the hell is arugula?*

Mark told me how cheap houses were in the Cities. "You can get a really nice place in a good neighborhood for only $150,000," he said, and I just stared. My little Duluth house, which had cost more money than I ever thought I would ever spend on anything in my whole life, had cost $35,900. Clearly, the Cities were not for me. I drove home, called Len, and told him no.

Len called a third time. This time he offered me a job that he said he had custom-designed for me. The title was senior editor, and it was a very good job—writing most of the cover stories for the magazine, editing the travel section, and commissioning and editing smaller freelance pieces. I opened my mouth to turn it down, and I found myself hesitating.

If I took the job, it would mean leaving the newspaper forever, and leaving daily journalism. It would mean leaving Duluth. I loved my little house on the edge of the woods. I loved the balance of magazine writing and fiction writing and newspaper work. Of my nine siblings, I was the only one left in Duluth, and my parents depended on me.

To complicate matters, the Thurber House had offered me a fellowship, and I was leaving in June for three months in Ohio. If I accepted Len's offer, it would mean going from Duluth to Columbus and then immediately to the Twin Cities. I would have to sell my house and find a place to live in the Twin Cities from a distance. Adventure was clearly beckoning, but I wasn't terribly adventurous. I would still have been contentedly working on the night copy desk if I hadn't been flung into reporting against my will. Still, I thought, maybe life was trying to fling me again.

So I asked my editor. She was a quiet, interior woman

who did not waste words. I was pretty sure that she respected my work, but I didn't know how she felt about *me*. I suspected that she saw me as too talky, and a bit flighty, and perhaps a bit full of myself, what with fellowships and part-time hours and freelancing. But she also had a remarkable ability to see things that I was slower to see.

I told her my dilemma. "Should I go, or should I stay?"

Linda didn't hesitate. "If I could, I would push you out the door."

On a gorgeous blue and green day in early June, I packed my car to leave. I hauled my summer clothes and a couple of boxes of books down the stairs and heaved them into my Toyota, and then I whistled for Toby. He raced down the front steps, and then he stopped, and I stopped too. Down my quiet street came a deer. Nervous and graceful, it picked its way along the blacktop on slender legs, stopping just at the edge of my yard. In my years in this little house I had seen black bears at my bird feeder, had heard coyotes barking before sunrise, and once, the year of the Halloween blizzard, had watched Toby run away after a red fox. But deer had been shyer, spotted only from a distance deep in the trees.

The doe stood for a moment, a minute, and then it turned, flicked its white tail, and bounded back to the woods. I slid my house key under the front mat for my summer tenants and opened up the hatchback. Toby jumped inside, and we headed out.

·

Epilogue

....

It's been sixteen years now since Toby and I
drove away from my house at the edge of the woods. In
those sixteen years I have slowly come to think of myself as
a St. Paulite, although not exactly a Twin Citian, and Duluth
still feels like home. No other place will ever settle in my
bones the way Duluth has.

Toby and I spent three happy months living in the attic
apartment of James Thurber's childhood home in Columbus, Ohio, where I wrote and Toby had several encounters
with the resident ghost. Just before Labor Day, Joey flew
out to accompany me on the drive home. But home was no
longer my little house by the St. Scholastica woods; it was
now a triplex next door to a SuperAmerica gas station on
a busy corner in St. Paul, rented sight unseen. We packed
up my rusty Toyota once again, Toby hopped in the back,
and we headed West. A too-brief summer of reading, writing, thinking, and teaching was about to be supplanted by
a new job in a new place, and I was, quite frankly, scared.
When I saw the bold skylines of Minneapolis and St. Paul
looming before us as we drove up Interstate 94, I realized
just how different my life was going to be. No longer would
I lie in bed and hear the coyotes barking in the woods, or

walk to work in a snowstorm, or write fiction in my spare time; now I would be living with the concrete and traffic of a big noisy city, and I would not have much spare time at all. For months, whenever I heard a train whistle blow down the street from my house, my first thought was that it was a boat signaling the Aerial Bridge.

I told myself I would forgo fiction writing for a while and devote myself to journalism. As it happened, I have forgone fiction and devoted myself to journalism ever since.

The glorious job created just for me at *Minnesota Monthly* lasted a year. Then Len Witt left, and with no one else to do the work, I stepped into the role of interim editor, planning the magazine, commissioning freelance pieces, writing very little, editing a lot. Every month I hoarded plum assignments, thinking I could write them myself, but, too busy, always had to assign them at the last minute to long-suffering freelancers. I kept hoping to return to writing, and the publisher kept promising he was on the verge of hiring a permanent editor, but after ten months I realized that nothing was going to change unless I made it change, so I quit and took a job at the *Star Tribune* in Minneapolis.

That day in the spring of 1996 when I interviewed for the position of social issues editor was revelatory; though it was my first time inside the *Star Tribune* building, the newsroom felt so familiar that I wasn't the least bit nervous, and I was certain that the job was mine. It had to be; newspapers, like Duluth, were in my bones. I spent a long June weekend in Duluth—where it was so cold that I had to wear mittens on the Lakewalk—and started at the *Strib* almost two years to the day since leaving the *News-Tribune*.

Since then, I've worked all over the newsroom—as

social issues editor, writing coach, enterprise editor, projects editor, and now books editor—and I've watched the
room change. You've seen it, too. Newspapers have been in
a slow, sad decline for years, fighting those forces that I only
glimpsed back in the Duluth days: advertisers seeing other
options and going elsewhere; the rise of competition and
instant news with twenty-four-hour cable channels and the
Internet; the decline of circulation and space. And the more
they decline, the more newspapers cut, and consequently
the more they decline.

Across the country, some newspapers have folded. Some
are just skeletons of their former robust selves. And others,
like mine, have weathered bankruptcy and come through
leaner and more innovative. The *Star Tribune* is constantly
experimenting with new ways to convey information, producing a midmorning newscast for the Web, building a
state-of-the-art video editing studio, and equipping staffers
with digital tape recorders and mini–video cameras. We are
all over blogs and Facebook and Twitter, and we are getting
used to doing video stand-ups, and God help those of us
who have what is known as "radio hair."

It's anybody's guess if these changes will save the *Star
Tribune*, or will save any newspaper. And everyone *is* guess-
ing (and posting their guesses all over the Internet). Me, I
keep my head down, do my work, enjoy the hubbub and bus-
tle of the Daily Miracle, and fervently hope it lasts. When
big news happens—Paul Wellstone's plane goes down, ter-
rorists fly into the Twin Towers, the Interstate 35W bridge
collapses into the Mississippi River in a heap of concrete
dust and screams—nobody does a better job of coverage,
and there is no place I want to be but the newsroom.

I don't think back all that often to the days of scanner paper and old guys in fedoras, but when I do, it is with great fondness and with a feeling of enormous gratitude. What a break it was the day Mrs. Hyvarinen suggested I try newspapers. What a break it was when the first newsroom clerk quit, paving the way for my hire. What a break it was when the editors decided to push me off the copy desk and into reporting. It has been a fortuitous career all the way through—begun by accident and continued through enormous amounts of energy and passion, and a huge amount of luck.

•

Acknowledgments

MEMORY IS SLIPPERY, AS MY FATHER USED TO SAY, AND so this book, while based on my recollections of eighteen years at the *Duluth News-Tribune*, is also bolstered by newspaper clippings, letters, old notes and photographs, and many, many interviews, conversations, and e-mail exchanges. It is as true as I could make it. I made nothing up—which should be a given, but in this age of problematic memoir perhaps must be stated outright.

Most quotations are remembered but not invented. Some are verbatim, taken from old letters or newspaper stories. When possible, they were verified by other people involved. Nobody seemed the least bit put out by being contacted out of the blue after twenty or thirty years and shaken down for memories of Duluth: everyone was delightful and extremely helpful.

Warm thanks, in particular, to Jacqui Banaszynski, who saved clips and memos and letters and shared them generously; Paul Brissett; Larry Fortner, who opened a lot of doors for me back in the day; Ruth Hammond; Jim Heffernan; my mother, Patricia Hertzel; Bob Jodon; Joey McLeister, who happily took part in many of these adventures, from the Iron Range to beyond the Iron Curtain; Pamela Miller, who saved hundreds of letters I wrote but now probably should go ahead and shred them; John and Ann Myers, for endless kindnesses (and their daughter Maggie, for giving me her bedroom); John Rott; and Keith Thomsen. Thanks also to my St. Scholastica lunch buddies, Patricia Hagen, George Killough, Tom Morgan, and Tom Zelman, and to Brooks Anderson, Ann Bauer, Amy Goldstein, Marjorie Hudson, and Andrew Krueger.

Sincere thanks to Patricia Maus at the Northeastern Minnesota Historical Center at the University of Minnesota Duluth for offering so much help, often at the drop of a hat (or an e-mail). She was invaluable. And to the staff at the Duluth Public Library for their great files, accessible (if seasick-inducing) microfilm, and friendly help. To Todd Orjala at the University of Minnesota Press, who liked this book from the start but then gave me a heart attack by telling me it had to be longer . . . much longer. The readers of Three Dog Blog were the first to love these stories about the early days and kept asking for more. Well, here it is: much more. Thanks to my bosses at the *Star Tribune*, Nancy Barnes, Rene Sanchez, and Christine Ledbetter, who allowed me time away from work to write one book only to have me come up with this book instead.

Enormous thanks to Ellen Akins, who is not just the best friend a person could have but the best reader too. Thanks to my other readers: Jim Foti, who is much more than a copy editor but is, frankly, one hell of a copy editor; Lynette Lamb; Peg Meier; Amy C. Rea; and Ralph Wyman. To Patti Lynn Hertzel Flores, who was so tickled that her cousin was writing a book. And, of course, my husband, Doug Iverson, who walked the dogs, listened to my stories, and made me laugh every single day.

Take a bow, all of you. You guys are the best.

Laurie Hertzel grew up in Duluth, Minnesota, and now lives in St. Paul with her husband and dogs. She is coauthor, with Mayme Sevander, of *They Took My Father: Finnish Americans in Stalin's Russia* (Minnesota, 2004). She is the books editor at the *Star Tribune* in Minneapolis and has won many awards for her journalism.